ENDORSEMENTS

Wow. What a page turner. If you're looking for adventure, a melted heart, more understanding of those who grieve, and a just-plain-great heart-felt story, *When Sunday Smiled* is it! This book will impact any and every reader with greater trust in God, comfort regarding any loss, and a sense of empowerment for life's challenges.
—**Kathy Collard Miller**, speaker and author of over fifty books including *No More Anger: Hope for an Out-of-Control Mom* www.KathyCollardMiller.com

This book is brave. Not an action-hero, I-can-take-on-the-world, my-strength-will-save-me kind of brave. It's a real kind of brave. A look-someone-in-the-eye-while-you-tell-them-you-love-them brave. A what's-left-when-I-got-nothing-left brave. A tear-soaked brave. This journey is full of unique characters and an ever-approachable wry wit and never becomes anything other than deeply authentic. I read it slowly, sometimes with a grin and sometimes with my heart in my throat and my hand over my mouth. What a walk. *When Sunday Smiled* is joy and heartache and grief and miracles—an unchallenging read that absolutely challenged me, and it's a book I'll want to revisit every time I need to be reminded what's important. I can't recommend it enough.
—**Kaley Rhea**, author of *Turtles in the Road* and *Messy to Meaningful: Lessons from the Junk Drawer*.

A thru-hike of the Appalachian Trail is an emotional life changing experience. Andy Davidson's life had already experienced upheaval before taking one step on that famous trail from Georgia to Maine. If you enjoy pure adventure you will enjoy *When Sunday Smiled*. However, this book transcends adventure. Not only is it a journey on two feet but a journey of the heart and mind as a father tries to comprehend the tragic loss of a son.

Where was God when my son died? That answer was revealed to Andy as he neared the end of his Appalachian Trail hike.

—**Paul Stutzman**, author, *Hiking Through. One man's journey to peace and freedom on the Appalachian Trail.*

In his compelling memoir, *When Sunday Smiled,* psychologist Andy M Davidson wrestles with God on the Appalachian Trail much like Jacob wrestled with God by the Jordan River. Trying to cope with the loss of his first-born son, Aaron, Davidson hikes the A.T. to work out his grief and the faith-conflicting emotions that pile on. This telling of one man's physical, emotional, and spiritual pain on the 2,190-mile hike from Georgia to Maine is raw and heart-wrenching. From white blaze to white blaze [the painted rectangles marking the trail], Davidson learns to recognize and appreciate God's creation, purpose, and provision. Like Jacob, Davidson's "limp" serves as a holy reminder: "For I have seen God face to face, and my life is preserved (Genesis 32:30)." I highly recommend *When Sunday Smiled.*

—**Clarice G. James**, author of *Party of One, Manhattan Grace,* and *Doubleheader.*

With deep insight and honest transparency, Andy invites his readers to journey alongside him on the Appalachian Trail as he chronicles his struggles around the loss of his son, and as he questions God's faithfulness. While it is his journey, he has captured the emotional instability that accompanies the heartache of grief experienced by many after the loss of a loved one. His book, written in vivid, expressive narrative has intrigue, adventure, inner searching, discovery and the revelation of God's faithfulness. *When Sunday Smiles* is a book that will speak to many hearts and propel its readers toward a better and more peace-filled tomorrow.

—**Janet K Johnson,** author of *Grief, the Unwanted Journey,* pastor, mentor in spiritual formation

Akin to Cheryl Strayed's *Wild,* coupling a grueling trek and devastating grief, Davidson's account takes a fork in the road, as he is not grieving the death of a parent, he is grieving the unexpected death of his beloved son, Aaron. This Gold Star mom resonated with the grief and despair of the unexpected death of a son. I also resonated with his expression of how the presence of God brought him joy and hope and healing along the way. The rich descriptions of his trek and the story of his anguish kept me captivated, I felt as though I was hiking alongside him. With faith, grit, determination and the steadfast support of his loving wife, he treks on, honoring his son's life.

—**Marilyn Weisenburg**, author, *Empty Branch, A Memoir: Finding Hope Through Lament*

Since Peter Jenkins invited a nation into his *A Walk Across America* in 1979, adventure-loving readers have waited for another storyteller who could guide us into the heart of our country and culture. Andy Davidson's book *When Sunday Smiled* does just that as he shares glimpses of beauty from the Appalachian Trail and introduces us to the colorful cast of characters he encounters along the way. But Davidson takes us on a richer, more profound journey than one defined solely by location and people. He also pulls his readers along a grueling expedition through his own deep grief and ultimately brings us out and into a new perception of the father heart of God.

—**Holland L. Webb**, content writer and editor, co-host, "The Afterword Podcast"

WHEN SUNDAY
SMILED
walking through life and loss

Andy M Davidson, PsyD

PUBLISHING THE POSITIVE
ELK LAKE PUBLISHING INC
Plymouth, Massachusetts

Cover and Interior Design: Derinda Babcock

Editor(s): Susan K. Stewart, Deb Haggerty

Author Represented by Credo Communications

PUBLISHED BY: Elk Lake Publishing, Inc., 35 Dogwood Dr., Plymouth, MA 02360, 2019

Library Cataloging Data

Names: Davidson, Andy M (Andy M Davidson)

When Sunday Smiled: Walking Through Life and Loss / Andy M Davidson

184 p. 23cm × 15cm (9in × 6 in.)

Description: After the loss of his son, Andy Davidson set out to walk the Appalachian Trail from Georgia to Maine, hopeful the trek would help him overcome his grief.

Identifiers: ISBN-13: 978-1-948888-94-3 (trade) | 978-1-948888-95-0 (POD)

| 978-1-948888-96-7 (e-book.)

Key Words: Hiking, Grief, Family, Relationships, Friendship, Healing, Inspirational

LCCN: 2019933934 Nonfiction

DEDICATION

To my wife, Lori, whose youth is reflected in her eyes, her beauty in her smile, and her fragile strength in her faith.

CONTENTS

FOREWORD

You could say I am the most grateful man in the world for having a wild dream come true, for making an impact, and for having the most wonderful family I could imagine having. If I ever lost one of them, I'm sure it would take me over the edge, and I can't even imagine the grief, pain, and anger that I would experience!

In his masterful book *When Sunday Smiled*, my former student/athlete Andy Davidson shares with us the grief he and his wife, Lori, experienced when their worst fears were realized … the unnecessary death of their son. It's an incredible story of going from anger to forgiveness to faith with nature as their caregiver and advocate.

I am not surprised that Andy was able to tackle the biggest challenge of his physical and spiritual life by backpacking on the Appalachian Trail. You see, I was Andy's coach in high school. He took on the trail, and healing, just like he took on every challenge I threw at him when he was a teenager … with grit, determination, and passion. Andy is a beacon to all of us who have forgotten how to forgive. His words are the perfect game plan for spiritual invincibility!

—Vince Papale, former NFL Philadelphia Eagle, author,
inspirational speaker and subject of Invincible, the movie.
VincePapale.com

ACKNOWLEDGMENTS

First to my trail partners and to my trail angels who nursed me, fed me, picked me up, and put up with my woes, my whining, and my fitful snoring. Y'all blessed me beyond all measures.

When my sister-in-law Clare heard I wrote a book about my 2,198-mile wilderness experience, she didn't hesitate to volunteer to be my first editor. I have the good fortune to be related to someone who was an English major in college. Clare lost her daughter at the age of eight to influenza. Clare worked tirelessly to turn my words into a manuscript. "Andy," she said, "We are part of a club no one wants to be a member of."

Susan K. Stewart fine-tuned my manuscript into a finished product. Because of her, I am a better writer and person. She is more than my editor, she is family. I was leery of turning my baby over to a total stranger, but she raised my manuscript as if my words were her own.

My brother-in-law, Dave, who devoted hours away to build my website at andymdavidson.com and kept me focused on my message.

The next person I must acknowledge is my publisher, Deb Haggerty, the head of our family at Elk Lake Publishing Inc. After sending her my manuscript, I was astonished to get an email the next day:

> Dear Andrew,
> We lost our son to an auto accident when he was twenty-four. Each parent's anguish and reaction is different, but I can empathize with what you and your wife went through. I would like to read the balance of your manuscript before I make a contract decision.

I sent her the final thirteen chapters and three and a half hours later I received a second email:

> Andy,

> I loved the book (I read the manuscript straight through—I read fast) … I am confident I will offer you a contract. If you have questions or would like to chat, call (after ten a.m.) or email me.

I suggested 10:01, but we settled on 10:30 so Deb could have her coffee.

I am blessed with three children, two who are still on this earth. Aaron had the heart of a cowboy, Ali has the heart of a mermaid walking, and Rob will always have a heart of gold. They have been our source of encouragement and inspiration. After their older brother died, they put the pieces of their lives back together. Lori and I gave our children roots, but they were blessed with wings and continue to spread them. There were times when I just wanted to give up but seeing them prosper amidst tragedy kept me going.

Also, our grandson, Jayden. I was on the phone with our daughter when I heard her say, "Jayden, it's Uncle Aaron, he died." Jayden continues to show us how to live and laugh again. His great-grandfather was right when he said, "Andy, that boy will be the best thing that ever happened to you."

We are blessed with a growing extended family, who have all prayed and worked to build a platform for my message. They have stood by us in our darkest hour and believed in me. Without our family and friends, you would not be reading these words today. I count them all joy!

We breathed a little easier when Aaron turned thirty. Parents do that. The days of skateboarding on the edge of a highway and snowboarding through thick pines were behind him. Almost thirty-one, our son had grown up and settled down. So we thought.

CHAPTER 1

No Regrets

Lori held my hand. In the early hours of March 30, I took my place in a line of travelers waiting for the Greyhound bus at a nondescript gas station/convenience store. Some hoped for a new job, others looked for a new life. I looked for a change. We stood together in the darkened parking lot in New Bern, North Carolina. I was the little kid trying out for the big kid's team. And the big kid's team was at Springer Mountain in Georgia, the start of the Appalachian Trail.

"No regrets," my wife whispered in my ear as she handed me a small pack of trail mix and some Jolly Ranchers. Her words sounded like something Adrian would have whispered to Rocky, but not something my wife would

say. I expected her to say, "Have fun, good luck, or hurry home." But, no regrets? Lori's message sounded strong, sounded powerful—sounded like something that I needed. I made those words my vow. *No regrets*, I repeated, *no regrets*, as I made my way to the middle of the bus. *No regrets*.

The problem is I regret everything. When I raised my hand at my Navy commissioning over twenty years ago, I stated, "And I do this with no mental reservations." I lied. I don't even walk to the bathroom without mental reservations.

Regret defined me. So, as I sat alone on the bus watching Lori drive away in the darkness, I had a lot to think about.

I scanned the bus looking at my new companions, who were also looking for a new chance somewhere along the line. They looked too big, too old, and too casual in out of style and faddish attire. I easily judged people, put them in boxes, and often looked down on them. We were headed different places, but we were together, bound by more than an aluminum bus. The next nine hours on the Greyhound were my first lessons in grace as we traveled down the same road.

By the time we pulled into Durham, I was comfortable in my seat with no one next to me. I ate most of my snacks before we picked up more travelers. As they made their way down the aisle, I avoided eye contact to protect my space.

The woman across the aisle cursed into her cell phone while holding a baby with the other hand.

"We're not doing this here!" she yelled.

Actually, we are. In fact, we are all doing this here.

After a stop in Charlotte, I got back to my familiar seat in my temporary home as we headed to Georgia. *What are you trying to prove?* The question came back as the highway miles rolled under the wheels of the ungainly bus. The question, asked several months before, rang in my ears as if my friend Dave was right next to me.

I needed to prove I could do it, whatever "it" was. Not everyone can walk 2,189.2 miles in one year. The Appalachian Trail Conservancy or A.T.C, estimates that only one-in-four will complete the hike from one end to the other—a thru-hike. An accurate count is difficult. Many people skip sections but still consider themselves thru-hikers. I believe the count is less than ten percent. I wanted to be a ten-percenter.

I wanted to walk off my grief like Earl Shaffer in 1948—the first thru-hiker. After returning from World War II, he walked from Georgia to Maine to walk off the war. No one thought a thru-hike was possible until Shaffer. Since his feat, over ten thousand people have hiked the trail in a calendar year.

My grief was born on a warm Sunday afternoon in North Carolina. I had just finished painting a small wooden boat when a local police sergeant with a flat-top military haircut walked up our overgrown stone path. He opened the wooden gate, looked around, and hesitated.

"Excuse me, Mr. Davidson?"

Did I do something wrong? Puzzled, I wiped the grey paint from between my fingers.

"I ... regret to inform you ... son ... motorcycle ... sometime this morning ..." His voice faded as he handed me a scrap of paper. "Here's a number to call. I am sorry for your loss."

My question was "why." Why has no answer. Why did God let Aaron die? *Why? You could have stopped the tragedy. Why didn't you stop that minivan?* Why? As a Navy officer, I knew when a ship runs aground the captain is responsible regardless of who is at the helm. *God why aren't you accountable for Aaron's death?*

"Why" drove me to depression for almost a year after Aaron's death. Depression is anger turned inward, and I was furious. I am a psychologist and a Christian, but psychology came up short, and religion followed close behind. I needed more. I needed real. I turned to the trail.

My goal was to finish the trail. "If you don't finish you are nothing," said a fellow hiker. At the time, I thought he was right, but finishing isn't everything. Nine hours on a bus increased my resolve to walk the trail as I promised to never get back on a Greyhound before Maine.

It was dark by the time the innkeeper met me at the bus station. I loaded my pack in the back of her aging Suburban and got in with a thirty-year-old lawyer-turned-barkeeper from New Orleans, also determined to become a thru-hiker.

"I hike a lot," she said, "but nothing this big. I hope my pack isn't too heavy ... I don't think I forgot anything, did you?"

"I hope n—"

"Do you have AWOL's book?"

"I'm gonna carry parts of it," I said.

"Oh. I have the app."

We had nothing in common but the trail, which proved plenty until we arrived at the Hiker Hostel. "Breakfast at 7:00," was the last thing I remembered before falling asleep.

THWACK! A canvas bag for linens landed on my shoulder and slid off the side of the bed. I woke to the sting of canvas.

"Huh? Wha ...?"

"You're snoring so loud."

"Wha ...? What?" I asked, dazed.

"You're snoring so loud," he repeated in an Irish brogue.

"Oh, I'm so sorry," I stated in my 'tired brogue.' "It's a real problem. Good thing you're not my wife, right?"

My new roommate didn't laugh. I heard him roll over. I checked my phone in the early hours of March 31. The hostel system along the trail is an inexpensive way to get a hot shower and a real bed, and a hostel was a good way to begin my hike. It's a case of "you get what you pay for" and in this case, he got to pay to sleep next to someone who snores too loud. I got to sleep next to someone who hit me in the middle of the night with a canvas bag.

I lay on my stomach, hoping anyone else who was still awake would fall asleep, and maybe I could get some sleep. I was in a large room in the basement of a log cabin. My roommate and I were the only ones in the room but there was another group of hikers in the next room. I just wanted morning to come; I wanted to be a thru-hiker.

Beginning at Springer Mountain in Georgia, the Appalachian Trail traverses through the Appalachian Mountain chain until the terminus at Katahdin Mountain in Maine. That last two-tenths of a mile of the trail is special, but I focused on the first of over 165,000 three by six-inch white blazes—  painted rectangles that mark the trail. I wanted to see my first white blaze at the summit of 3,780-foot Springer Mountain in north central Georgia.

I stayed away from the Irishman at breakfast the next day. I wanted no bad will coloring my walk. I ate as much as I could, weighed my pack, and climbed into a cramped van to the approach trail. I wanted to be in the woods to rid myself of the grief toxins that pulsated through this fifty-seven-year-old body. I wanted to be a NOBO, a North Bounder, to walk in one direction for the entire trail route. "Blue Blazers" take alternate routes that bypass mountains marked by "blue blazes" on the trail. I didn't start this venture to hike the Alternate Appalachian Trail, the A.A.T. I was there to hike the A.T. "Yellow Blazers" skip large sections of the trail by getting rides. They pass the yellow lines on the road to keep their hike alive.

"Flip Floppers" often start in the middle of the trail in West Virginia, go north to Maine, then drive back to the middle and walk south to Georgia. Flip Floppers get the benefit of better weather but lose the continuity of the trail and the camaraderie of the other hikers. That was too complicated. I hiked north. I carried everything I needed on my back. I walked looking for one thing—the next white blaze. That's what I did. I walked.

I stepped out on the eve of the busiest day of the trail and the birthdate of my youngest son. March 31, and I was in the middle of the "the bubble," when most hikers go north. My adrenaline rushed as I hurried past disillusioned hikers ill-prepared for the challenge. The trail contained all shapes, sizes, and configurations of backpacks. Backpackers resembled crazy cars from a Richard Scary children's book with cups, shoes, tents, and sleeping pads dangling from over-stuffed shells strapped on hunched-over backs. I breathed heavily through the early miles and passed hikers whose dazed stares of bewilderment mixed with a hint of helplessness.

"Fine," was always their weak reply when I asked how they were, but their eyes betrayed them. Their eyes conveyed, "What did I do?"

Stopping for lunch at the first shelter, eight miles along the trail, I met a large hiker. He was bent over, holding his back with one hand while the other hand gripped the edge of the picnic table.

"My Special Ops instructor in the Army always asked me why I carried so much weight. I used to carry a hundred pounds," he said.

I doubted if he was in Special Operations, but I didn't question him in his pain. His contrite partner clutched his hamstring and lamented how he thought he was in better shape. In the background, his wife, on her cell phone, tried calling for a shuttle ride back to town. I didn't know there was a shuttle or a town. I didn't want to know and pressed further.

I was hurting too. From the beginning my knees hurt, more so when going downhill. On the first day, I cursed aloud, then prayed as I staggered down a large hill. Six months didn't give me enough recovery time after my orthoscopic surgery. Because of my brief recovery, I only did ten training hikes of various distances along the North Carolina coast. The only hill I faced was a bridge. I trained on flat and short courses compared to what I would face in the upcoming days.

My lunch of salami, cheese, and flat bread seemed adequate when walking beach miles, but the Appalachian Trail is no beach. Worry crept in as I walked away from the impromptu infirmary at the shelter. I pressed on.

Before he died, Aaron and I talked about hiking the two thousand-mile, five million steps of the Appalachian Trail. July 27, 2014, changed everything. In the fall, after I spent my workdays staring at my computer, my company asked for my resignation. By January, I didn't recognize the desperate and bearded old man in the mirror. Lori said I'd feel better if I cleaned up. She filled her time with pictures, friends, and flowers. At night, I listened to her sobbing. Nights were forever.

I read how the Appalachian Trail is life-changing. I watched videos of people persevering in the wilderness, alone in their thoughts, surrounded by the night. They walked a simple life. I wanted that. No, I needed that. I was dying inside, if not dead already. I wanted to die. I didn't want to kill myself, but I wanted to be with Aaron. I was running away from something, but I was running to something. What, I didn't know. In the mountains and miles, I would find out. After losing Aaron, I would find me. I had to do something. I had to get up—I had to walk.

Along with researching the trail, reading books, and talking to anyone who would listen, I started a blog before I left. My blog became a source of motivation as my growing group of readers developed into a support group. I needed them, and I prayed for them thinking what I would write as I traversed the next six miles. An early blog entry I entitled "Sleepwalking":

> For the last seven months, I've been walking in a haze, "sleepwalking," a therapist friend called it. I like that. Grief will do that to you. Robbed of happiness, devoid of joy, missing a reason to go on. Not sure if I want to live or die, just knowing I need to put one foot in front of the other. I'm afraid. I didn't want to sleepwalk the trail. The number one rule, every thru-hiker knows it, is HYOH, Hike Your Own Hike.

After fourteen miles, I settled into a site alongside Justus Creek. I set up my tent, ate the first of five months of Knorr noodles and tuna, and climbed into my sleeping quilt.

As I slept, a soft rain woke me from my sleep and I realized, "THAT DUDE HIT ME WITH A CANVAS BAG."

After eighteen hours and fourteen miles, the Irishman who woke me because of my snoring at last touched my anger. Too tired and too far away to do anything.

Let it go. I fell asleep to the harmless patter of rain on my nylon tent. *Let it go.*

My first morning on the Appalachian Trail meant the start of a routine that repeated itself for the next five months: let the air out of my sleeping pad while lying on it, pack up my clothes and sleeping bag, make breakfast, then break down my tent.

Breakfast consisted of Mueslix which must mean "mush" in German. I read online that Mueslix is high in fiber, but I didn't read German mush tastes like hay seeds and wallpaper paste. Fiber is good, but I couldn't eat mush for the next week. I ditched the rest and broke camp after eight as I headed towards Neel's Gap to buy more supplies.

At the end of the day, I found a stealth site halfway down a water trail. Stealth camping is pitching your gear at a site not established by the A.T.C. I later found out that it's frowned upon because of the mark stealth camping leaves on the wilderness. The official sites where backpackers corral after a long day of hiking miles through the wilderness are good for safety and good for the environment by decreasing the impact on the trail. I found a site barren of vegetation and other humans. As the sun went down, my fear went up. There are a few fatal incidents that are now part of the Appalachian Trail lore. When I shut my eyes, visions of Jeffrey Dahmer danced in my head.

In the morning, I hiked back to the trail. Rock music blared from a tent at the intersection.

"Hey, I'm Sparrow," the bearded thirty-year-old said when he stuck his head out of his tent. Sparrow looked like a young Elton John and seemed too happy for so early in the morning. Still shaking out the cobwebs, I pretended a greeting and kept moving.

Blood Mountain loomed ahead. The climb was as intimidating as its name. While I climbed at a strong pace, the younger, stronger, and more experienced Sparrow blew by me. On the first day, Mountain Squid told me, "It's not a race, the last one to Katahdin [the end] wins." Mountain Squid is a retired Navy Chief who volunteered to count thru-hikers. Thru-hikers had trail names. I was still looking for mine. Squid is a negative label for a sailor, but Mountain Squid turned squid into a good thing. Well, I was winning as Sparrow's pack disappeared into the green canopy.

Alone in my thoughts, my mind drifted home. Lori told me she needed her time alone. Although she had backpacking experience and felt comfortable in the woods, she had no desire to hike two thousand miles. Her first child's death left her vulnerable. She needed familiar, she needed home on the North Carolina coast. The ocean's ebb and flow brought certainty, and the warm beach under her feet grounded her. Watching the sun set off our deck gave her hope. Her garden, her friends, and intentional butterflies gave her security.

The trail was well-suited for reflection and meditation. The footsteps of so many hikers wore a gully lined with rocks, roots, and mud. Even without the white blazes painted on trees every hundred yards, the wear made the trail discernable until you came to an intersection. When other trails intersected, I often went wrong. The repetition of my footsteps put me into a hypnotic trance that allowed for reflection and for getting lost with regularity. The physical exertion, matched to my rhythmic breathing, freed my soul to transcend the trail. I drifted to God, to family, back to me, to my fellow hikers on the trail of life, and always to my son.

Still early, I stayed dry, fed, and healthy, but as I hiked uphill, a fog surrounded the crest of Blood Mountain. A solid stone shelter stood at the top as a testament to the Civilian Conservation Corps. The CCC was part of the New Deal that Franklin Delano Roosevelt instituted to help lift the country out of the Great Depression. Across America, evidence of the CCC remains in National Parks and monuments as beautiful stonework and significant infrastructure from highways to dams.

It was easy to imagine the workers lifting huge stones and carrying the massive amounts of concrete, wood, and hardware for food and a few dollars in their pockets. Content to have a job, they worked to get themselves and this country back on its feet. Today, the shelter was an impressive structure with a huge chimney. The foreboding stone building's door was locked, leaving me to look in a windowless opening from the cold and damp.

CHAPTER 2

I Have A Plan

I sweated in the drizzle. I could go further if my Gore-Tex boots kept my feet dry and I stayed warm. With little prodding I moved on towards Neel's Gap. The physical pain and repetition from walking gave me a certain amount of clarity for the emotional pain of my loss. I wrote in my blog:

> While hiking, my mind often goes blank. In the rain, I realized
> tears rolling down my cheeks. Every day tears will happen. Today
> I dwelled on the 27th of July. Where was Jesus on the 27th?

Jesus was there on that fateful day when a woman driving a minivan pulled out from a golf course into the path of my son's motorcycle. He was there. He lifted my son out of the carnage of that tangled mass of steel and rubber and took him home. My boy rose on the twenty-seventh of July 2014. Now, my son is home.

I had a shaken faith but a faith none the less. Most of my life, I believed in a loving God. As a psychologist, I had a career attesting to bad things happening to good people. I thought I knew what they were experiencing, but I fooled myself. I knew nothing. Now my hurt overwhelmed me, and anger consumed me. The hole left where Aaron used to be—will stay.

I stepped out in faith to fill the hole with hope. My hope was that Aaron is with God, protected and perfected. The trail gave me the space to talk to the one I was most angry with—God.

WHEN SUNDAY SMILED

I cried stepping into the rain on Blood Mountain. My significance was humbling and my humanity reassuring. Through the haze, God and Aaron were there—they just had to be.

I felt broken and dead—I didn't care. I wasn't in a fog. In fog, you put your lights on, slow down, and keep going. Not a tornado–too defined. You can hide in your bathtub from a tornado. I was underwater while everyone else was poolside. I tried to talk, but no one heard me. They wanted to, but they couldn't, not when I was underwater. They weren't with me. Just because they came to the pool didn't mean they were in the water. Just me. I didn't know what they were saying. Somewhere underwater, I could see Lori, and together we reached for each other.

On July 27, almost a year prior, I slowly climbed the stairs to tell Lori the police sergeant's message.

"It's Aaron." She saw it in my face.

"He's gone," I said, looking into her innocent eyes.

"What? What do you mean gone? … What do you mean gone? Andy, are you kidding?"

"No," shaking my head. "He died. In a motorcycle accident."

Lori fell down. I wanted to lift her up, but I stood watching this fragile mother, her blond hair spilling around her, as she pounded her tears into the wood floor.

"No, not Aaron, no." Helpless, I knelt next to her and put my hand on her back wanting to help. Minutes drifted. She got up.

"I'm sorry, so sorry." I blamed myself, but I didn't know how to fix it. I had nothing to do with his death, but guilt racked my body. I thought I was going mad, but I wasn't crazy—I was a parent. We held each other in disbelief.

With tears in her translucent blue eyes, she asked, "How?"

"I don't know," I said, wiping mine.

Lori looked lost. "Where?"

"I'm not sure."

"When?" Getting her words out between breaths.

"Today, morning, maybe?" I wanted to be sure, but I wanted to be wrong.

"Are you sure? Please, no. Are you sure? Not Aaron, NO." Her voice echoed in my ears.

Back on the trail, I was in a real fog. My pace quickened as I hiked down the 4,461-foot mountain to the outfitter's building at Neel's Gap. Two stone CCC buildings straddled the trail, connected by a covered porch. Overhead, an electric line ran from one of the buildings, and old pairs of hiking shoes hung on the line, giving testimony to a myriad of ill-prepared hikers who had left the trail.

I dumped the contents of my pack on the floor inside, while the outfitter told me what I might need and what I should send home. I hadn't overpacked. He suggested a larger water container and a pack cover to keep my gear dry. Despite spending over a hundred dollars on a pack, my reinforced nylon didn't keep my down sleeping bag from getting wet. My biggest fear was being cold and wet at night. I paid the thirty dollars for a piece of nylon to keep my sleeping bag dry and my fears at bay. Some things are worth more than the price.

Sparrow walked out of Neel's Gap hostel holding a pizza fresh out of the oven in one hand.

"Staying here?" he asked.

"No, hadn't even thought about it," I replied. *It's early, and he hiked so strong, and now he is staying here?* Sparrow liked hiking, but he liked hostels more. Sparrow claimed to hike all year long due to his family's financial independence. The name, Sparrow, was fitting because he flitted from place to place. He said he hiked from the Florida Keys to Georgia and planned to hike into Canada after he reached Maine, just not today. Today, after hiking five miles, he ate pizza.

I left the outfitters and hiked up the next hill thinking about Sparrow's pizza. After a few days of hiking, walking uphill became easier than downhill. Uphill is good for the heart; downhill is bad for the knees. The weather started clearing, but as I climbed, turned wet again. With a twinge of regret, I thought about the dry hostel at Neel's Gap.

The weather looked ominous as the hours ticked away faster than the miles. Checking my guide, I found Whitley Gap Shelter, a mile off the trail. A rookie mistake to go so far, but I needed water, and I needed dry, so down I went. Way down, until I arrived at a three-sided wood hut with a metal roof that blocked the wind and raised the temperature a few degrees.

Alone in the dark, my mind drifted to my oldest son, a self-made cowboy. Aaron sneezed as a child whenever we put him on the back of a horse. But there he was, a grown man standing in line with a bunch of kids before getting up on a slab of leather wrapped around a metal barrel. Our snowboarding, skateboarding, downhill biking, motorcycle riding son slid off a lethargic mechanical bull in slow motion well short of seven seconds. We just laughed.

"I'm still gonna ride a real bull."

"Please, Aaron, PLEASE don't."

My words meant nothing. I told him not to be reckless on his skateboard when he was a teen. He skated off the roof. He just had to.

He never got the chance to ride a real bull.

His Phillies ballcap was his cowboy hat, his Harley was his horse, and the ski mountain where he worked, his range. Like all cowboys, he lived by a code. He bought American, listened to classic rock, and read classic novels. He played hard and worked harder. He'd go to town with his "boyz," but he was at home on his mountain. We didn't own our cowboy—nobody did.

The only thing that owns a cowboy is his code: when it's broke, fix it; when it's wrong, right it; and when it's hurt, take care of it. Cowboys are quiet; they are content; they have an inner security and an outer hesitancy. Their morals run deep, but they are their morals and no one else's. Oft wary of the total stranger, and sometimes gruff, but if they needed help, they were no longer strangers, and he was no longer gruff. Yesterday a memory, tomorrow a notion, today is all they have. They live in today. I wanted him to spend his youth in college and strive for the next promotion like I did but he had other ideas. Aaron had thirty years of todays while the rest of us live in tomorrows.

Thing is, cowboys die. Sometimes they die young, and sometimes, they die hard. Aaron was dead, and so was I.

Now in a darkened shelter, the only light came from my cell phone. With one bar on my phone, I connected with Lori and lamented on my third night. I was lonely and wanted company.

"Lori, I can't believe you can hear me. You sound so close."

"I am close," she laughed.

Lori laughs, smiles, and goes out of her way to be friendly. No one really knows her vulnerability, inner strength, or her deep sensitivity. Her smile hides her hurt. I'm the daydream believer, and she is the homecoming queen. We are from different worlds. When I met her, I knew I could never let her go. Complementary opposites, we grew on rocky soil to complement each other.

"How do you get to be homecoming queen?" I once asked.

"You just have to be nice to people."

Way too hard.

Because of her smile and warmth, even her friends don't know how fragile she is. But she knows. Lori fought her fragility with forty-five minutes of weights and aerobics. "It's the only thing I can control," she said. Lori has her mother's laugh that covered her tears. She hides her tears until she meets another mother who has lost a child, then she takes on the mother's pain as well as her own. She was Chicken Little in her grade school play, but now her sky really was falling.

Not a moment after we hung up ...

"Hey!" boomed a voice out of the darkened rain. I startled, seeing two older hikers: Sleepy, tall and lean, and Grumpy, short and athletic. Grumpy was anything but and Sleepy suffered from insomnia. The two experienced hikers piled their soggy gear onto the dusty wooden floor. God reached out to say, *Andy, I have a plan and you are in it.*

If the sun shone, and my feet stayed dry, then my faith stayed strong. As soon as my feet got wet, my mood soured. When the terrain turned difficult, my optimism turned downward. Sleepy and Grumpy had walked twenty-five miles for each of the past two days. Twenty-five miles was a marathon compared to my paltry thirteen miles.

They shared their experiences and their rations as we talked into the night. The next morning, the clouds separated to reveal a beautiful day. I tried to keep up with Grumpy but stayed with Sleepy who'd incurred a bad case of blisters from walking so far in the rain. Because of Sleepy's blisters, they pulled up short at the next road where they made their way back to their car. Despite his agony, Sleepy tried to share his gear with me. I declined but pressed on to Trey Gap buoyed by their support.

Trey Gap was an innocent piece of real estate before Trey Mountain, marked by a stone road. I set up my tent in a secure spot next to an RV advertising candy bars and cold beer A few hours after I climbed into my sleeping bag, the heavens opened, and the rain fell in biblical proportions. I don't know if the rain, the thunder, the lightning, or the wind scared me the most.

I prayed like Jonah in the belly of a whale. All night I prayed. I wondered if the only thing holding down my three-pound tent in the forty mile-per-hour wind was my 165-pound body. After the water filled the bottom of my tent, my sleeping pad looked more like a float in the middle of a kiddie pool. I tucked my down-filled quilt around me to prevent the down from getting wet. Wet down is bad news because the feathers lose their ability to retain heat and takes days to dry.

In the middle of the storm, I crawled out of my tent. The howl of the wind was maddening. My tent held its ground. My food hung from a tree in a small nylon bag known as a bear bag that looked like a Halloween dummy blowing in the breeze. Life makes me hungry and fear makes me famished, so I got my food bag. Reasoning I would save time in the morning, I found a protein bar to eat. I would not die hungry.

A repeat performance could have driven me from the trail after only three days. *Three days? I can't go home after three days.* I pictured my nine-year-old grandson Jayden looking up at me and saying, "You quit?" I can't quit just yet, and besides, there was nowhere to quit. Greyhound doesn't stop on Trey Mountain. Good thing too.

CHAPTER 3

Just Walk

Just before sunlight, I broke down my camp, put on warm clothes and left Trey Gap. I struggled to pull my gloves over my cold stiff fingers before I hiked up the mountain clad in my foul weather gear. Blood returned to my legs and feeling returned to my fingers. I felt ever so happy to have a good pair of Gore-Tex gloves. A pair of gloves, a piece of hard candy, or a brief word of encouragement—these little things had huge meaning when I had so little.

A tall, lightly bearded hiker walked toward me. Surprised to see someone else out at this early hour traveling in the opposite direction, I asked, "You hiking the A.T.?"

"Yeah, trying to get to Maine."

"You know you are going south?"

The hiker explained he'd used the privy and thought he was still on the privy trail.

"No, you're on the A.T." This quiet man turned around and followed me north. We were the same age, with the same goal of thru-hiking, and his trail name was Soil.

"Soil, like dirt?" I asked.

"No, SO–IL, 'cause I'm from Southern Illinois."

"I'm Wizard," I countered. *Soil? We have to do something about that.*

Everyone has a trail name on the Appalachian Trail, and from the beginning, people asked me for my trail name. The best trail names are the ones given to you on the trail, but most people invent one for themselves that has nothing to do with the trail. On my first day, a hiker asked me for my trail name, so I said, "Mobic," which is the name of the anti-inflammatory drug I take for my knees. She looked puzzled. Mobic had about as much cache as Soil.

The next time someone asked, I was Wizard. Wizard is what the Marines call their psychologist because when they went to see the wizard, sometimes they didn't come back. Wizard can be a term of endearment or a term of reproach.

Wizard I was, Soil was my new trail partner, and true north was the direction. After a few miles, the sun burned away the last remnants of the grey-clad sky. At Addis Gap, we read a colorful sign pointing to eggs, bacon, muffins, and beer.

"Muffins?" I asked.

"Beer?" asked Soil.

It lay a quarter mile off the trail. Along the way, we met two hikers coming towards us.

"Too far," they stated.

I looked at Soil. "Muffins."

"Beer," he repeated, and we kept walking downhill.

I won't walk a quarter-mile for a waterfall or even a view, but I will walk a quarter-mile for food—and further for free food. On the trail for four days, food already took a greater significance than I had heretofore experienced. In the past, food was sustenance. Now, when I walked miles with a small apple pie in my pack, that apple pie became my main motivation to make my goal.

On the trail, I couldn't just get off the couch and reach into a freezer for a half-gallon of ice cream, so I started to fill my mind with thirty-one flavors. When someone offered me something as simple as a fun-sized Snickers bar, I blossomed with inexplicable gratitude. Food took on a spiritual meaning. Food was evidence of God taking care of me. At the end of the day, I never tired of a foil packet of tuna and Knorr noodles, never. Just remarkable.

We traversed the quarter-mile to one of the finest "trail magic" spreads of my entire journey. Trail magic is a random act of kindness that befalls a hiker. Someone handing you something you lost several days or miles ago, or someone giving you a ride into town are trail magic. Sometimes coolers are left along the trail filled with sodas and snack cakes. Hikers crave Coke. Coca-Cola to a hiker is like crack to a junkie. Finding a cooler with the last Coke is divine, but finding a cooler with the last empty Coke is almost demonic.

The people providing trail magic are trail angels. Some angels spend their lives taking care of hikers. Others become angels by doing the right thing at the right time. Both make the A.T. special. They filled me with a renewed sense of confidence, not in myself, but in humankind. They reassured me I was okay. God provides through creation, and humans are at the pinnacle of that creation. When I stood on mountains and looked over vast valleys, or at night when I stared at the stars, I felt small but significant. Last night, fear took over, but today, I was secure.

Kind-hearted trail angels carried in crates of food and even a keg of beer, north of Trey Mountain. Time of day is irrelevant for beer and hikers. Dehydrated, I gravitated to Gatorade, orange juice, and Moon Pies. Oh, and muffins. The morning was amazing—no, miraculous—that I was sitting on a log, eating eggs by a warm fire, surrounded by angels and hikers. A few hours ago, I was miserable and fraught with fear. Now I felt fat and happy. Moon Pies—miraculous, just miraculous.

"The trail provides" is a trail mantra, but God provides the trail. God is good. Life? Life is hard. Life is hard for everyone, but harder for some. There's a T-shirt that says, "Life Is Good." My wife loves the saying. Well, life can be good—but life is hard. Life is hard for the woman with cancer. Life is hard for the mother whose sons are in jail for murder. And life was hard for the dad when a police officer came to his door on a Sunday afternoon telling him his son was dead.

※ ※ ※ ※ ※

"I ... regret to inform you ... son ... motorcycle ... sometime this morning ..."

His words grew faint. My world slowed. Sunday slipped away. Dazed, I looked at the path and thought about that overgrown grass between the stones. Aaron was two thousand miles away; we just talked to him two weeks ago. *How can he be dead?* We had our best talk in years when he told me about breaking up with his girlfriend. He was soulful and open. He went his own way when he graduated from high school, but now, he was close to family and me. And now he was gone. *Dead?* Dead confused me like Opie on *The Andy Griffith Show* holding a dead bird but wanting it to fly away. What did I care about that overgrown grass? I wanted Aaron to get up. I wanted him to fly.

WHEN SUNDAY SMILED

I held onto the scrap of paper the sergeant gave me. The number of the Jefferson County Medical Examiner in Colorado—my only proof—was scribbled on the paper. I called the examiner and again, "Mr. Davidson, I am sorry for your loss." I wondered how many times I'd hear those words from friends, family, and strangers. Everyone seemed sorry, but no one could help. They couldn't make it better; they couldn't bring him back. A minivan had turned into a missile when she turned in front of our son's Harley. That minivan took my life too.

We called our youngest son, Rob, in Afghanistan, who arranged to get back to the States. Rob was taller, leaner, and younger by almost four years than his brother. The two teased, joked, and fought like brothers. They were as different as their looks; Rob found ways to interject himself in conversations while Aaron avoided them. Rob's sensitive side could be demonstrative while Aaron's was an enigma. As a child Robby could cuddle for an hour—Aaron for a hot minute.

And then, I called our middle child, Ali. When Robby was born, she took to her younger brother like a little mother and followed her older brother like a tomboy. Now she had a son of her own and put herself through college before the two moved to Colorado. Ali and Aaron lived an hour apart from each other. Being a military family, we raised our children with wings. Our children proved their independence by striking out on their own.

While on the phone, I heard her say to her son, Jayden, only nine, "It's Uncle Aaron ... he's dead ... Jay, Uncle Aaron's dead." Aaron was the one man who took time for the little guy. *God—what God?*

Lori and I stared out the window. She embraced his picture, and I embraced my tears. Friends surrounded us within the hour. The look in their eyes confirmed it. Aaron was gone. Women talked, and men stood outside on the deck. Dave made plane reservations, Bev took our dog, and Dixie planned to drive us to the airport the next day.

We took the first flight to Denver and drove to Keystone Ski Resort where Aaron had worked. Lori and I must have talked, at least a little. We held hands during the day and held each other's tears at night. Nights lasted forever. At one point I broke down, sobbing so loud I scared Lori, who rushed to hold me. We were alone together and lost apart. We occupied the same space, but we still had to go through our grief separately.

We cried over his beautiful body in a mortuary with a mortuary smell. His life now snuffed, stolen, and lifted from us. For weeks, I shut my eyes and still saw Lori lying prostrate, pounding her fists into the tear-stained floor.

The trail is tough, but life is tougher. But life isn't bad, either. Life just is. "He makes His sun rise on the evil and on the good, and sends rain on the just and on the unjust"[1]. It rained on me. It rained on me last night; life rained on me last July 27, and the rain will come again. Today the sun shone, and my belly was full. Today, I had a quiet partner who listened to me chatter how I almost got blown off the gap. And how much I like Moon Pies.

The trees wrapped themselves around rocks in search of water. The smallest bugs hovered around my exhalations and landed on the leaves and branches before me. Seeing the rain gush down a trail, the sun providing life, and the stars that light the way spoke to an unremitting God. These forces worked together from the smallest bug to the largest star. Surrounded by God's beauty, I succumbed to his evidence—everything has a purpose, everything a home, even if it's a rock for a bug to rest on or for the Son of Man to lay his head. There is a plan for everything, and today my plan meant hiking the trail, meeting hikers along the way, and opening myself to possibilities.

We needed to resupply, so at the next road Soil and I got a ride to the Top of Georgia Hostel. The hostel workers gave us hospital scrubs while they did our laundry. Dressed alike in baggy pastel scrubs and sending us into town together gave us a cult-like appearance.

Sparrow showed up at the hostel with a pair of female hikers, who smiled to hear I was as scared as they were during the rainstorm a few nights back. I joked about other hikers I met along the way. Everyone laughed. In the past, the attention made me feel good, but now my sarcasm left me hollow. *Is my sense of humor changing too?*

I resupplied, took a needed shower, and got back on the trail. My confidence increased when Soil and I crossed the Georgia state line and crossed our first hundred miles. My goal to average twenty miles a day was unrealistic at the beginning. My spirits lifted getting through the first of fourteen states. My first hundred miles took forever. But now I straddled the trail between Tennessee and North Carolina.

My journey took me to the top of Mt. Albert, the tallest point in North Carolina. Albert at 5,250 feet amounted to my toughest climb to date. Still not in the best shape, I slowed while Soil climbed stronger than I could. My meniscus tear and orthoscopic surgery less than six months ago meant being out of shape at the onset. I struggled to the top of another grey-clad mountain despite stopping several times as my partner ascended the rock-strewn path. This mountaintop had a fire tower, but I kept walking.

Thoughts of how far I still needed to go to get to Maine proved daunting. I tucked them away and concentrated on a precious lesson: Just walk.

That's it—just walk—regardless how far I had to go. My knees throbbed. Just walk. I was tired. Just walk. I was hungry. Okay, just eat. My son is dead. That one just sucked. But again … just walk. Just walk summed up my most important lesson. In the military, I worked with the Marines who said, "Just shut up and color," but that's not what I did. I kept going but I couldn't shut up. I began talking to other hikers and strangers I met along my trek.

There was no one to take me home if I quit. There was no one to pick me up when I fell on the rocks at Mt Albert, and no one to drive me home at night when I missed my wife. There was no one to dry my tears when I reached each summit, and my eyes welled with happiness. I got up, took up my cross, and followed him. I walked. When people learned of our loss, they wanted to help. Some offered advice, some offered support, some offered help. But I was still alone in my grief … so I walked.

After Mt. Albert, we walked strong to another mountain, then headed to Franklin, North Carolina. The monotony of the A.T. lies in stark contrast to the towns that punctuate the trail like commas in a run-on sentence. Franklin is famous for its friendliness. A shuttle bus piloted by Ron Haven greeted us on the dusty shoulder of Route 64 bisecting the trail. His gregarious Mr. Haney-like demeanor from the old sitcom, *Green Acres*, gave me pause. With me still early in the hike, with only 111 miles of wear on my boots, Ron's part salesman, part trail angel delivery struck me as incredulous.

Really? You are giving free rides and not asking for anything, really? You are this friendly? We don't have to stay at your hotel or hostel, and you will take us anywhere in town?

After climbing in the bus with a dozen other hikers and packs, I spied a picture of Ron advertising his run for commissioner. His Franklin pride oozed as he gave his well-worn version of the town's collective history and offerings. My wariness was unwarranted.

Hiking the trail from Georgia to Maine, I expected a variety of environments that tore at my resolve. I didn't expect the variety of people like Ron who built back my resolve. After checking into the motel with Soil, we scurried across the busy road to eat at a Mexican restaurant. Coming out of the woods after two weeks, our senses were dulled to the mechanized world. The dizzying pace of the cars and people crowded out the quiet of the woods.

Later, Ron drove the hikers to an outfitter's store and to Walmart. After sharing the washing machine and just before falling asleep, I remember telling Soil how happy I was hiking with him, and he agreed.

The next morning, I was even happier eating a free pancake meal at the First Baptist Church. Just glorious. A woman took our pictures and mailed them back to our families. Gratitude that strangers could be that thoughtful filled my heart.

After Ron shuttled us out of town, I climbed the next of many inclines with tears in my eyes. I had been closed to the world. Strangers, even friends, got pushed to a safe distance. Now, my hike started to become a pilgrimage. Franklin softened my heart and whispered in my ear, *God has a plan, and he still cares.*

A green canopy covers the rocks of the Appalachian Trail. The shade created a false monotony as one muddy trail choked with roots turned into the next. Heights occasionally gave way to cleared peaks. Brief vantage points revealed a vast eastern wilderness.

The imposing Tennessee landscape of succeeding ridges and corresponding valleys testified to the resolve of its pioneers who carved out a life in a pre-mechanized era. Descendants continue to forge a way of life, which echoes independence and self-determination. The people of Franklin helped me on my way.

Funk joined Soil and me as we headed out of town and walked to Rocky Bald. Funk was a few years older but in good shape due to leading an active retirement in the mountains of Utah. His short grey hair and wire-rimmed glasses added to the stern look of a former federal inspector. Funk was short for his last name and served as his trail name. We looked back and saw Mt. Albert in the distance from the next observation tower. The mountain seemed so far. We'd hiked far in a short period.

Dang, I can do this.

When we met youngsters handing out snacks, they asked if we were thru-hikers. I hesitated. A thru-hiker is someone who hiked the entire trail in one year. A thru-hiker is what I wanted to be;but a thru-hiker wasn't what I was, not yet. I didn't want to jinx myself, so I explained, "I'm not a thru-hiker yet, but I am thru-hiking."

Just as I couldn't call myself a thru-hiker, I couldn't call my partner Soil any longer. Soil sounded too much like dirt, and he deserved better. Greg was quiet and unassuming, and always deflected any attention or compliment. He looked like Fes Parker, the actor who played Daniel Boone on an old television show, so Funk and I began to call him Mingo, Daniel Boone's Indian sidekick. This lasted two days until we met someone along the trail who asked him his trail name. "Ah … Just Greg," he replied. Soil washed away, Mingo faded, and Just Greg survived. The name Just Greg fit his humble persona.

I grew tired of my trail name as well. Beneath my pack, my sweat soaked back felt every pound of the shifting weight, and my chest heaved from the deep breaths. Near the crest and out of breath, I hung my head when I asked Funk how much further.

"You're the expert," came his reply.

"Excuse me?" My head snapped to attention.

"You're the one with Clinical Psychologist in front of your name," he retorted.

Maybe he had a problem with psychologists, or maybe he was also tired. I walked away and didn't talk to him for the rest of the day. I wanted a trail name that came from the trail and not from my past. He told me I was too sensitive. My sensitivity helped me relate to people, but my over-sensitivity caused too much pain. More than a name change, I wanted a "me" change, or at least a major overhaul. I continued to walk.

CHAPTER 4

Chaos

I made concessions to hike in a group. I had a romantic picture of being the lone mountain man bushwhacking my way through fourteen states. I dreamed of fending off the elements, foraging for nuts and berries, and the freedom to be me. But a group offers good conversation, and it's fun to work as a team. With a group, I stopped when I wanted to go further, walked when I wanted to eat, and slept in a hostel when I wanted to camp. A group distracts from the number one rule: Hike Your Own Hike.

Funk talked us into staying at the Nantahala Outdoor Center, so we pulled up short. He liked the feel of a real bed. The NOC is North Carolina's version of a Colorado whitewater town. Kayakers, rafters, bikers, and hikers converge at the NOC.

We ordered lunch at a rustic restaurant along the river filled with kayakers playing in the rapids. When I walked across the restaurant balancing a drink and a salad, a crouton rolled off the plate. I stared at the crusted cube now on the floor. An hour ago, I would have picked up the crouton from the dirt and eaten it. Now I passed on the morsel, knowing I could always get another one. It didn't seem right.

As we watched the kayakers dancing around the gates in the water, I couldn't help myself. I teared up as I imagined my two sons splashing each other and making fun as they flipped each other's boat to be first. "What fun," I thought while making my way to the bathroom for tissues and space to be alone.

After falling asleep, I dreamt of being back on the farm in Pennsylvania with Aaron and his grandfather. Aaron loved working with his Pap the farm equipment together. Pap sweated and cursed like a farmer while Aaron laughed and held parts for his mentor. Life-perfect. Is it a dream when you wake up and your life is the nightmare? Life-perfect would never be the same.

So I hiked farther. After leaving the NOC, we walked modeling a bicycle paceline in the Tour De France. I saw more of Funk's heels than the surrounding woods. At the next road, we ran into two young hikers with big plans. They stood around a bag of huge red apples left on the picnic table by a trail angel. Chef was the personal chef to a wealthy family, who vacationed in Europe for the summer. He was out of shape and looked like he brought along half of his kitchen on his back. His cheerful manner boarded on naïvety, and his extroversion made him good company. If he stopped talking, he'd likely pass out from a lack of oxygen.

"I skipped thirty miles," he said, "But I can still be a thru-hiker as long as I hike two thousand miles."

The problem is he'd hiked less than two hundred miles and already had skipped thirty. Each year, the mileage changes slightly due to maintenance or the acquisition of wilderness, but the trail has always been greater than two thousand miles. If you hike the whole trail, you get a patch that signifies you are part of the two thousand-mile club, but Chef had his own definition. As we walked away, he was still talking to Eagle Feather, a young hiker from Colorado.

"What a loser," Funk said with disgust as we walked away.

"He's not a loser," I responded. "He's not a thru-hiker, but he's not a loser."

I identified with my fellow hikers. I liked Chef. He was young and great at his job. He wasn't great at hiking.

"I bought my pack because it's blue," Chef joked, "and I bought my tent because it matched my pack."

Funk also disparaged Eagle Feather who had a refreshing fun-seeking attitude. Whoever he met, Eagle Feather treated like his best friend.

"Hey, Brother Man," Eagle Feather said, smiling through his missing teeth. He called everyone "Brother Man." Eagle Feather thought he could walk over twenty miles that day despite the time being noon already. He reminded me of my son's friends in Colorado. I liked how he accepted me at face value, and he deserved the same. Maybe he wouldn't hike twenty miles, but he would have fun trying.

"See ya later, Brother Man."

We headed up the long, straight, and rocky climb known as Jacob's Ladder. I sweated, then sweated more. Just Greg and Funk waited for me at the top.

"I'm getting better," I said between breaths.

"You are," Just Greg assured me. Still not there, but I was getting in shape. We spied a good camping spot on the top of a small hill that already had one tent. Funk and I waited at the base of the hill with Just Greg's pack while he walked up to the tent.

"Hello," he called into the tent.

"Who are you?" replied the female voice.

"Just Greg. We're thru-hiking and want to camp here."

"You don't look like a thru-hiker. Where's your backpack?" She had a point.

"Well, I am—my pack is with my friends. We'd like to stay here tonight."

"I guess so," she conceded.

As we set up camp and made dinner, she watched from inside her tent. After a while, the female hiker from North Jersey drew closer. Wanderer, a retired postal worker, carried mace, "and it isn't for the bears, either," she reminded us.

Despite the difficulty of the trail, we were getting closer to the Great Smoky National Park. Along the trail, the hikers spoke of the Smokies in epic proportions. From the Smokies to Maine, rumors abounded. I learned to decipher fact from fiction. The Smokies has its fiction but the fact is the weather can be severe. Hypothermia is a real thing. Since being on the trail, I'd beefed up my forty-degree quilted down bag with a thin silk liner and a nylon bivvy sack to keep the inside dry. My sleeping system was light, adjustable, and multifunctional: the attributes of an ultralight hiker. If I got too cold, I would wear socks, long underwear, and Aaron's ski cap.

When I packed for the A.T., function and weight were the only two criteria. But I wanted to take something along that my son owned—as a reminder he was with me. Aaron was happiest working and snowboarding at Keystone Ski Resort. Now I had his hat that kept me warm, even in the rain. I told no one, not even Lori, about something else I carried—a plastic pill bottle with some of my son's ashes.

The Smokies in April are nasty. Known for the cold, the Smokies' wet weather and gnarly roots choked the trail. Hikers and fog clung to the muddy trail. Hikers have a healthy fear of the Smokies for good reason. Walking out of Georgia was my first benchmark—walking out of the Smokies would be next.

The most visited national park lay between me and Fontana Dam, another Civilian Conservation Corps project. Displaced workers built the massive dam in the 1930s bringing electricity to the Appalachians while their families built a way of life. This brought opportunity to mountain folk, but a simple way of life was lost. People relied less on their neighbors and grew more skeptical of God.[*]

Because of the crowded Smokies, we were required to buy a permit, so rangers would know when we entered the park in case we disappeared along the trail. Someday they may restrict the numbers but for now they just collected data. We deposited part of our hiking permits into an overstuffed box neglected by the understaffed Park Service. I shoved the other part into my cargo pocket, thinking once I was in the mountains, life would get easier. For this day, life was easier. The weather cooperated, the forest was beautiful, and my spirit grew strong.

After fifteen miles, Funk convinced us to sleep in a crowded shelter. I made the mistake of telling the person next to me to poke me if I snored too loud.

"That's enough!" I stated after I got my second poke for the night. I laid there staring into the darkness. *I am not an animal,* I screamed inside my head.

Rain fell most of the next day. We saw no vistas, only gray "smoke," which gave the park its name. The trail got more difficult due to the rain and the worn-out roots. Because of the wet, I found myself in another shelter. Funk agreed to sleep next to me to be my bodyguard in case anyone else couldn't take my snoring. Trail Blazer, an older hiker who completed his thru-hike in 1979, lit a fire in the fireplace. Six Strings, an eighteen-year-old German hiker, soulfully strummed his ukulele.

After being wet, smelly, and miserable all day, I was warm, fed, and burrowed in my down sleeping bag. Pure peace, a mellow version of joy. The music and fire were every bit of magical. Again, I felt a curious feeling—

gratitude. Despite minor differences and concessions, I connected with my world, a brief respite from the despair of the past year. Turmoil and anguish floated up the chimney with the smoke from the fire. My caustic emotions would be back, but for tonight my grief was harmless smoke in the night air. I fell asleep knowing I was surrounded by good people.

The Smokies were unique for their age and their ecosystem. Along the trail, massive trees had toppled, and now, instead of leaves, green moss grew on their bark. One tree was so big that when it fell over, the roots clutched a boulder as big as a VW. The power of life and death surrounded me as I walked through the decaying forest. Shrubs and saplings, with a will to live, grew between the rocks, while mighty trees would get pushed over in the next storm.

Everything connected and influenced the other. And everything seemed to affect me. I stopped to touch the rough bark and the soft moss. I stopped to smell the decaying forest. I breathed in the fresh air in the middle of the rain. My senses were so strong that I teared up. I saw, heard, touched, and smelled everything as if for the first time. I felt like Scrooge reborn on Christmas morn. I became part of my world and I liked it. A lot.

But I didn't like the climb up Clingman's Dome. Not as tough as Jacob's Ladder, but the climb was up … and I was wet. I sweated inside my rain jacket and my Gore-Tex boots got soaked from my wool socks, which turned my mood sour. Later, I learned to hike in the rain in just a synthetic T-shirt and shorts but not on this day.

Clingman's Dome observation tower is a spiraling concrete ramp that accessed a saucer shaped vantage point. The tower looked more like something out of an episode of the Jetson's space-age cartoon. I took a picture of the futuristic-looking edifice that stood juxtaposed above the natural foliage. After waiting for Just Greg to come down the tower, I bent down to adjust my pack. I must have taken too long because when I looked up, I found that my hiking group had left me. At first, I panicked. Then, I found out how much I missed going at my own pace—stopping when I wanted and moving on when I didn't.

The drizzle let up at lunch when I sat on the edge of a parking lot to make my salami and cheese sandwich. Out of the woods emerged Blurbon, an energetic retired Army colonel. His forceful manner exuded confidence. We walked to a road where a trail angel offered to take us down into Gatlinburg, Tennessee. I was wet, cold, and going to Gatlinburg—the tackiest town along the Appalachian Trail and likely east of the Mississippi.

We got a room with three single beds for Blurbon, me, and Miami Vice, an ex-vice cop from Miami. As loudly as Blurbon talked, Miami listened just as quietly. His soft-spoken Spanish accent put people at ease.

At an all-you-can-eat restaurant, I asked Blurbon how he got his trail name. He shared his testimony of despair and triumph of a past marriage. I told them my hike was a walk back to God after my son was taken from me.

I told them before I got on the trail, my springer spaniel, Belle, and I were training in the rain. After miles of soggy clothes and cold fingers, my burden grew heavy, and the tears on my face mixed with rain drops. During my training hike, I had my first glimpse that Jesus was there when Aaron's motorcycle careened into the side of the minivan. Aaron had done nothing wrong, but now he was dead. I told Miami Vice, I am beginning to see that God has a plan. I may not always like things his way, but Aaron and I are a part of them.

Miami told me he was forced to leave the police force. His quest to find God included meditating at a Buddhist monastery and completing a religious pilgrimage, "El Camino de Santiago," in Spain, which was featured in the movie, *The Way*. I still don't know how Blurbon got his name.

The next morning Blurbon and I shared a ride back to the trail with Misfit while Miami Vice stayed behind. Misfit's name seemed to fit him as he seemed out of sync in social settings.

The rain came down in a torrent; the trail spilled the overflow like a series of waterfalls. We were ankle-deep in water and mud, going uphill against the current. At one point, Blurbon fell off the side of the trail. I watched helplessly as he clawed his way back onto the trail.

Despite a late start we slogged sixteen miles in that morass. I stopped to make a soggy sandwich wrap on the side of a large stone.

"We won't make it," Blurbon said.

"What do mean?"

"We haven't even passed the first shelter," he stated.

"Yeah, we did, a long time ago."

"Are you sure?"

I doubted myself. "Yeah, I ... I think so." *Man, I hope so.*

Thank God, I was right. After a short time, we came to the second shelter. In the Smokies, all hikers were required to stay at shelters due to the aggressive bear population. With the constant rain, hikers began congregating at shelters and stopped hiking. Many of them zeroed for days, never leaving the dry roof, good company, and plentiful pot.

"Not me," exclaimed one hiker, "I didn't zero. I did a negative hundred. Yesterday, I camped a hundred yards north and came back here to stay." We stood in a circle of tired, wet, and oddly content hikers. And we laughed. Blurbon made me some hot soup to warm up my insides and my fingers.

Two hikers, one heavy, the other slight of build (named S**ts and Giggles), told hilarious stories of getting hit on in Gatlinburg and somehow, getting out.

Someone stretched out his hand holding a joint.

"Hey, Wizard, you want some?"

"No, thanks. I made it out of the seventies without smoking, so I don't want to break my record." I was beginning to think the name Smokies had nothing to do with the clouds.

"That's cool. How 'bout some of this?" offering a flask. I didn't know what was in the flask, but it warmed me up all the way down. I was happy to see the flask make a second round.

The shelter was built to hold sixteen people. That night, the small hovel held thirty-one: ten people in the loft, ten people on the first deck, and ten lining the floor. And one service dog. Dogs were not allowed in the Smokies due to the bear population. Unless her service dog filtered water or blew up a sleeping pad, its only purpose seemed to be to share the misery. I found out later that both owner and dog soon quit the trail.

Blurbon shared his tent which we pitched beneath the awning of the shelter for a most restless night. Despite sleeping at the opposite end, my snoring made getting up early easy for the both of us.

We broke camp at first light. Blurbon was eager to meet his wife that evening, and I was eager to leave the Smokies. Before we left, two young hikers stood under the roof sharing a joint. One had a guitar strapped around his neck.

The other asked, "Hey, man, do you think Janis Joplin would have been just as good without the drugs?"

Oh, my gosh, that's the same conversation we had in 1973. I guess the commercial is true—nothing happens when you smoke pot.

As we walked away from the haze, Blurbon remarked, "For a Navy guy, you hike good."

Blurbon's mission to get to Standing Bear Hostel to meet his wife propelled him forward while I picked my way down the mountain. I got stronger going uphill but going downhill still proved to be slow. My legs just didn't flex like they used to and the pounding under my knee caps was excruciating. *Just me ... just hike.* Down the mountain I hiked until I got to Standing Bear Hostel. Blurbon met me with a hug and a pizza. I bought a beer for him and a soda for me. I felt like I had escaped a war for which I was ill-prepared.

Standing Bear Hostel is one hostel with a must-see reputation. Built along a creek, it's an eclectic collection of rustic buildings with a flair for artisan talent. The hostel was stuck in a '60's timewarp. I rented a dusty bunk, then I got a shower and did my laundry at the same time. It's called "hobo laundry" when you wear your dirty clothes in the shower to save money. Hobo laundry doesn't work as good as a washer, but after the first hour on the trail no one cares.

With Blurbon returning home, Funk asked me to rejoin the group that now included two others, Weatherman and Beast. Just Greg was ahead on the trail. I had to retrieve my map I left back at the hostel, so I declined his offer. Not the first time I'd forgotten something.

Earlier, Blurbon had looked back at me and said, "Dude, you need to get a system."

"I have a system," I said. "It's called CHAOS." I figured that CHAOS stands for Christ Has All Operations Secure. My slogan sounded good, but he was right. I realized, *God's world opened when I decluttered my life so that everything I needed was on my back and my only concern was the next white blaze.*

Everything in my pack was essential, and I could not afford to lose one item. Over time and miles, I worked on my system. I liked solo hiking and struck out on my own. If I packed the same way every day, my system was my friend. Despite the best system, life happens. You can do everything right and still end up with a cop on your front lawn on a Sunday afternoon.

CHAPTER 5

Moon Pies

The trail jumped between Tennessee and North Carolina and headed to Hot Springs, Tennessee. But my pilgrimage headed toward April twenty-eighth when I would fly to Colorado to stand in court with the woman who killed my son. Before I left from home for my hike, I typed out a statement. Each time I rehearsed my speech on the trail, I ended up in tears, but as I rehearsed the words changed. Grace was taking hold and pushing anger out. *Practice grace* became my new mantra.

I found judging the seventy-two-year-old woman who pulled out in front of my son after dropping her husband off at a golf course easy to do. What she did was wrong. My son drove the speed limit, wore a helmet, and was obeying the traffic. She didn't take the time and failed to yield as she tried to cross three lanes of traffic to make a left turn. She could have waited, could have looked twice, she could have turned right. She didn't.

My son died on the road that day. All of us now live with it. She needed grace as much as me. If God could forgive me, then I could forgive her. For years, I counseled Marines coming home from the war to forgive themselves—to let go of the guilt that plagued them. My turn to forgive was next. I wrote the following in my blog:

> All along the way, sun, or rain, I am thinking more and more about the sentencing hearing in Colorado on the 28th. Sometimes I well-up with tears; often I think in amazement what could happen. I think of my family; how each are coping in their own way and again fill up with tears as they continue to

pour their support on me. Each day I am humbled by it. The A.T. is a trail of humility; I oft fail, but I get up and get going again. Thank God for his forgiveness. No regrets, none.

I cried every day on the trail—save one—probably because I was dehydrated. After a quiet and dry—yes, dry—night, I camped alongside a shelter. In the morning, I packed up my system and headed to Hot Springs. With two days of rainless weather, the first since I left Georgia, I headed into town. I invented something I called GFH—Gravity Fed Hiking—in which I shuffled along in a controlled jog. GFH was easier on my knees than trying to brake on the down hills. Also, I went faster. I don't think I was the first one to come up with this but, like Columbus and the West Indies, I claimed GFH.

Hot Springs was celebrating its Trail Days, a festival honoring the trail and its hikers. The town looked like a scene out of *Oh Brother, Where Art Thou* when three young blonde girls took the stage to sing a combination of gospel and classic rock songs. As I walked down Main Street, I ran into Six Strings after he won the talent contest with his ukulele.

"Wizard," he shouted in his German accent, "Look at my new hiking shoes."

He was so young and far from home, yet he was content. I didn't stay in town. I wanted to make more miles because I would be off the trail for a week for the sentencing hearing. After doing much needed foot care while sitting on the curb at the corner gas station, I gathered my supplies to leave.

When leaving, I came across the two young hikers I met in the Smokies, S**ts and Giggles. One of them was crossing the street with twelve-packs of beer balanced on each shoulder, "PBR, Wizard, PBR!"

Pabst Blue Ribbon is the beer of choice along the trail, and he asked me to join them at the local motel. I declined. Before I left town, I also met up with my old hiking group and gave Funk one of my Moon Pies. My offering wasn't much, but it was a Moon Pie. My attempt at grace.

Every trail town seems to be in a valley. The river carved out the valley, and as the town grew, the water attracted industrial growth. With each valley comes a descent into town and a steeper climb out. As I hiked up, a day hiker stopped me and held out his hand. He asked me if I needed one of these—a small plastic disc that keeps the pole from sinking into soft ground. They come in all shapes and sizes, but this one was just like the one I lost from the bottom of my hiking pole a few days back. I couldn't contain myself. I wanted to hug him. He must have thought I was losing it and, well, I hope I lose more of *it*, whatever *it* is.

That night, I slept alongside the trail. The next day, I hiked in the rain to a road where I found a wet coupon offering a cheeseburger special for five dollars at the Hemlock Hostel and Paint Creek Café. I pressed the soggy slip of paper between the pages in my trail guide as I pressed on to my cheeseburger. Now motivated for lunch, I hiked five miles up the road.

The name, Hemlock Hostel and Paint Creek Café, was longer than the restaurant was wide. I walked into the main room of the cafe. Three men and Mom looked up like I had just walked into their living room.

"Hello," I said after an uncomfortable pause.

"Yeah?" asked Easy Rock.

"Well, I have this coupon here."

"Let me see that," demanded Easy Rock, who wore a T-shirt and tie.

He scanned the coupon for the official stamp as if I'd counterfeited the paper to cheat them out of a bag of chips and a coke. I got a little indignant. I'd walked five miles in the rain motivated by trail litter, and now I was on the verge of being shut out on a technicality.

"Okay, it's good," he declared, and Mom made my cheeseburger.

As I ate, the rain returned in torrents. The weather convinced me to stay the night in the bunkroom where I met Dentist. Not a real dentist, of course, he got his name along the trail for filing down one of his broken molars with a nail file. Dentist worked as professional sailor in the Caribbean. We laughed for an hour as we compared hostel customer service stories.

"Some hostels know how to put the "hostile" back in "hostel," I told him. "When you add an "s" in hotel, anything goes."

Hemlock Hostel boasted a quiet set of buildings akin to Standing Bear Hostel. The food was good and the accommodations adequate, but hard times had befallen the establishment. Mom's husband, who started the hostel, had passed away less than a year ago, and a recent fire destroyed the home they built.

I walked back to the café at dinner time for fried trout. Easy Rock, still sporting his glasses, T-shirt, and tie, came over to my table with an order pad and pen.

"Would you care for dessert? We have molten lava cake, à la mode."

Mom peered at me from behind the counter.

"Is it good?" I asked

"How do I know?" Mom barked back in a raspy voice.

After her work was done, Mom said, "Everything we serve here is homemade."

The next day, Scout drove me and a father-son combo to the trailhead.

"You work here?" I asked.

"F-NO" came the thunderous reply.

"Okay, okay. I thought because you had driving privileges, you worked at the hostel."

"I'm just trying to help the old lady out," Scout said.

I left with a father/son team. They were slack-packing, and the father planned to take a blue route, an alternate, easier hike around a pinnacle in the trail. *Not me, never,* I thought as I climbed the difficult ascent. I was here for the real A.T., not the A.A.T. (Alternate Appalachian Trail). I started dry, but the rain returned. A pair of friends from Texas, the Wild Boys, offered their campsite, so I settled in for the night. One of the Boys was originally from Tijuana but is a Philadelphia Eagles fan like me. Now that was weird.

The miles were melting away as I passed the three-hundred-mile mark. Upper teens and twenty-mile days became the norm, marked with an occasional trail magic. At one such event, I met a hiker with a ball cap that said USMC and a camouflage pack.

"Are you a Marine?" I asked.

"No, but if it gets me a little extra, then I'll wear it."

I boiled inside, and with incredible restraint, I later found the words to confront him. After twenty years of working with sailors and Marines who served in war, I was incensed that this poseur would buy a hat to garner cheap rewards. He told me that's not what he meant, but I later saw him in Damascus with a new hat.

The next town was Erwin, Tennessee. In between the town and me were some incredible views. Each sunrise brought a new adventure. I was never a morning person—never. But going to bed at first dark and getting up at first light agreed with me. Sunrises and mountaintops brought tears to my eyes. I was lonely for the chance to share the moment with someone I loved. I longed for my son and worried for my wife.

Lori was already in Denver with our daughter, Ali, and our grandson. "I just don't get the point of this trial," Lori remarked. I had met with the district attorney and his assistants in the past year. Reliving the accident was just too painful for her. She would never forget her son, and she didn't need to be reminded of that day.

I walked down to Uncle Johnny's, my last hostel before I left the trail to fly to Denver for the sentencing hearing. Uncle Johnny's Hostel is run by Johnny—a bohemian, long-haired, heavy-set man in his sixties and from the sixties. The hostel was well-run and took a group of us into town for dinner. The well-run hostel left me behind in the parking lot. None of the other hikers noticed I wasn't in the van when they pulled away early.

Wherever I went along the trail, I was meeting up with people who didn't remember me. I felt left behind by my old hiking group, and now, I was left behind again. *Maybe I am forgettable.* I called Johnny, and he sent the van back.

Back at the hostel, I met up with Scout, who'd given me a ride a few days ago at Hemlock Hostel. He was looking for Miss Janet, a trail angel who was following the bubble to Maine. "The bubble" is the term for the largest number of hikers, and Miss Janet is the most famous of trail angels.

I bunked in another dusty room with wornout mattresses. Lobo bunked next to me. He wore an official USMC uniform cap with chevrons sewed on top. They are called "covers" in the military, and a Marine never desecrates his cover. Odd to see a Marine dressed this way.

Lobo sorted through his food while he told me he used his food stamps for his supplies. He started his hike last year but got off the trail due to an injury. He planned to restart his hike in Pennsylvania but missed the trail so much, he started early in Tennessee. Lobo stopped sorting for a moment, looked at me, and asked if I thought he should mail some of the food home to his kids.

Where do you start with that? I didn't know what to say and looked away.

I called a former thru-hiker named Coma from Uncle Johnny's. Two days prior, Coma staged a trail magic cook-out and offered a ride back to the airport in Asheville, NC. His trail friend partner, Three-Piece, showed up at the hostel the next day. Named for the Kentucky Fried Chicken combo, Three-Piece chattered on about starting a new social movement involving the trail, pot, and love. Guns might have been mentioned, but he could have been joking.

Three-Piece's previous thru-hike offered a level of meaning for which he longed. He had been a waiter but despised the fake customer relationship. I got to share my story how I am trying to trust God as he sees me through my grief. You can argue the existence of God, but it's tough to argue with a man who just lost his son.

"That's real, man," he said, before driving the rest of the way in silence.

A live and let live atmosphere permeated the trail. Church groups offered food, a ride, and sometimes a roof, which hikers wouldn't refuse. The church groups and the hikers both seemed to get a need met, but one group went one way and the other group went north. Pleasantries were exchanged, but little more. Despite having a faith, I felt a closer connection to my fellow hikers and could see how the churches tried but often fell short of connecting with our group.

I didn't know where to begin when I talked to young hikers without a spiritual foundation. I hoped my example of stepping out in faith was an example to get people to stop and think about a relationship with God and not deride him as a mere religion. But I needed a story that they could relate to.

Getting through three states—Georgia, North Carolina, and Tennessee—were milestones of the trail. I hiked almost three-hundred and fifty miles and was nearing Virginia—the longest trail mileage. I had my system, my trail legs, and my confidence. I continued to read the New Testament, and the concept of grace continued to jump out at me. Grace was Jesus's message.

Getting through the sentencing hearing on the 28th of April would be a bigger milestone. The event marked a clear line when our family was forced to confront the ugly realities that someone took our boy from us eight months prior. Grace is what I needed most.

CHAPTER 6

RAISING COWBOYS

A large relief map of the trail loomed overhead as I sat in the airport in Asheville. People ignored the map that was now my life. The distance left to hike overshadowed the distance already hiked. My three-hundred and fifty miles looked puny compared to the eleven states and almost two thousand miles left to go. I took a quick snapshot, but the map didn't even fit in the picture.

I began reading my new book, but I couldn't get the trial out of my mind. *Wild* by Cheryl Strayed is about a woman who walked the Pacific Coast Trail after her mother died of cancer. She told of her recovery and her quest to become whole again. I cried before I finished the forward. *I'm such a chick,* disparaging myself and most women. I cry—a gift of sorts. No longer was I embarrassed when others looked my way. It's biology: you blink, others yawn, I cry. That's all. I cry. I'm crying now as I write these words. My headphones are in my ears and Pandora just chose my son and his former girlfriend's song. I cry every time I hear it.

Lori met me after my plane touched down in Denver, and I was still crying, but I pulled myself together in a fledgling facade of strength. *I am not strong,* I thought as we made our way through the city to meet with our daughter and grandson, *but I need to be*. I needed to be strong to deliver our message to the court, to the defendant, and to Aaron's Colorado family. I needed real strength.

Lori smiled like always and hugged me like never before.

At the Jefferson County Courthouse, they ushered us to the Victim's Assistance Department. Bikers surrounded us wearing club colors on dirty denim vests, along with mothers holding babies, and people just caught in the throes of life. I recalled Aaron telling me how he avoided bike clubs on the road out of a healthy fear. I was even more judgmental, but on the trail, I was learning to suspend judgment—in the courthouse I practiced it.

Lori was never the judgmental type. The worst she could say about someone is, "They're not my favorite." She remained pleasant with the officials, quiet in the courtroom, and sociable with Aaron's friends from Keystone Resort. She was still skeptical about why we were there.

We met with the assistant district attorneys, Brian and Darren, who would handle the case. Patti, the victim advocacy representative, was an experienced, kindly soul who might have been five feet tall. Today, she invited the first witnesses on the scene to meet us. They wanted to meet us and share their story with us.

The husband, a former Marine, and his wife told us how the accident occurred, how Aaron had no time to react despite traveling at a safe speed, and how despite his effort to administer CPR, Aaron died on impact. Knowing our son did not die in agony or because of a medical or procedural mishap helped in some small measure. Knowing he died surrounded by good people who cared reassured us—these people made a difference. If anything, meeting them gave Lori some peace. I trembled meeting the people who helped Aaron.

After entering the courtroom, eight of Aaron's friends from Keystone Ski Resort surrounded us. His boys strengthened our confidence knowing he will always be loved. As a lift mechanic lead, in charge of a maintenance team, he loved his work, he loved his life, and they loved him. Aaron worked, lived, and played with his friends, who were his Colorado family.

❦

"See, Dad, we're like the military too," he'd said when he took me behind the scenes of where he worked. *You are better. Unlike the military, you won't leave after a few years, all of you want to be here. You love your team, and all of you are committed.* The military is made of good people, and I believed Aaron and his crew were as good as the best.

Aaron didn't care for structure. He respected the military, and people who went to college, but he could get bored in the classroom. Because of his strong SAT scores, I encouraged him to go to college. He had other ideas and at eighteen, moved in with his friends in a college town. I told him, "Don't sign a lease and don't co-sign a loan—ever." He co-signed a lease.

About the same time, one morning while sitting in a tree during hunting season, I called Lori and whispered, "I'm so happy up here." I was at her father's farm in Pennsylvania.

"That's great," she said. I think I woke her.

"No, you don't understand," I said, "I want us to move back here."

It took some work, but that's what we did while Aaron continued to live with his friends in Virginia. He called me one night after getting into financial trouble and some legal issues.

"Can I come home?" he asked.

"Yes, yes," I cried.

Our prodigal son came home to Pennsylvania, the place he loved. I handed him a wire brush, and he worked off his debt that summer by scraping and painting the barn roof. He sweated his transgressions away through the hot, hard, dirty work. Our kids were under one roof. Alongside his grandfather, Aaron started a new life. I heard him laughing to himself as he worked around the farm. When he told me he wanted to go to Penn College of Technology to study auto mechanics, I told him he wouldn't like it.

After going through the two-year program, he was a certified Ford mechanic. He didn't like it. One Christmas, we gave him money to take a ski lesson at Ski Round Top in central Pennsylvania. He didn't take the lesson, but he got a snowboard and lift ticket, and loved it. Aaron grew up on a skateboard, so snowboarding fitted him. While at the ski slope, he saw a notice that they were looking to hire a lift mechanic. *I'm a mechanic.* He applied and got the job. And he loved it.

When he started a long-distance relationship with a Colorado girl, he was torn between living in the state he loved and being with the woman he loved. The woman won. He landed a job at Keystone Ski Resort. Colorado is the major league of ski resorts. Aaron's boss told me that in his interview, Aaron punctuated his sentences with "sir," talked of growing up in a military family, and humbly discussed his mechanical background.

"He was a rising star, and we loved him," stated the CEO of the resort. After six years, he was promoted ahead of several others to Lead Mechanic. The lift on the back side of the mountain was under his supervision.

"He was special," Grant, his supervisor stated. Grant was more than a supervisor; he was a friend and a father figure. Aaron lived with his coworkers and played on a company ice hockey team. Together, they worked and snowboarded on the mountain.

Aaron developed a love of motorcycles. This might have started when I picked him up on my 185cc Yamaha Exciter and drove him home one and a half blocks on his last day of kindergarten. After he moved to Colorado, he bought a small Harley Sportster. The motorcycle fit him—a sensible bike at a good price. He promised his girlfriend to always wear his helmet in a state that didn't require one.

He worked all winter to rebuild his bike. He manufactured parts, rebuilt the engine, and made the Harley into *his* Harley. It wasn't a show bike, the bike was him: tough, modest, solid, and a big engine that didn't quit—ever. Now, he gave me a ride, and I was the kid.

I wanted him to go to college, get a job, and get married. He would have been miserable. He chose happy. Somehow, we raised a cowboy—a modern cowboy. He was allergic to hay, couldn't stay up on a mechanical bull—but he was a cowboy. Leery of authority, he longed to be outdoors and had a fierce sense of commitment matched only by a strong work ethic. His values were more conventional than mine. He loved classic rock and classic literature. His movie tastes focused on gangster movies and westerns: anti-heroes who had their own set of principles.

When we packed up his things after he died, seeing his taste in books and movies were my books and movies was both startling and humbling. Sitting on his night stand was a knife I gave him when he was twelve years old. He carried a Buck knife I gave him when he was sixteen on his work uniform. I now carry the small Buck knife he carried the day he died.

The day before he was to go on a motorcycle trip with Grant, Aaron took his bike to be dyno tested in Jefferson County, near Denver. He texted a friend saying he was twenty minutes away. He never arrived.

Now, I sat in the Jefferson County Courthouse. The defendant pleaded guilty to a failure to yield charge and a careless driving resulting in death charge. The latter charge carried an automatic loss of license for one year and a possible year in jail. She did not want to lose her driver's license, and her lawyer attempted to make a deal for a lesser sentence. They realized there would be no deal, and she accepted her fate—sparing everyone a trial by jury.

The woman's lawyer pleaded her case that the intersection was a difficult one and that she had a perfect driving record to date. He stated his plea wasn't an excuse—but he was not convincing. He further remarked that her children and grandchildren were here in testament to her character.

I thought of Aaron's friends who sat behind us. They were his brothers, a testimony to his character. The district attorney informed the court we only sought the loss of license for her act. Grant followed with an emotional statement, then Aaron's ex-girlfriend, then his sister.

Next was my turn. After almost a month on the trail and one week in Denver, I felt oddly secure and well-prepared. Earlier, I recorded the following in my journal:

> Well, I'm sitting in a Denver Library with people and traffic abuzz. Only three weeks-plus on the trail, and the world seems too fast for me. It's always been that way. My oldest [Aaron] was nick named "Slo A" because he talked slow and reacted with equal speed. Maybe that's why I liked being a psychologist, because I slowed the conversation to my pace. After a few weeks of woodsiness, I get a sense of the enormity that envelopes our world. Control is an illusion, closure is a crock, and now the trail moves along, regardless. Let it go, let it be, just let it go.

I stood in front of the judge, the prosecutor to my right, and the defendant seated to my left. I'd practiced my statement in my head so many times along the trail I didn't need to read, but my written words kept me on point. These were my words verbatim:

> "For God so loved the world that he gave his only begotten son."
> It was a warm, breezy, but sunny Sunday, late afternoon. I was just finishing the final details on a rowboat that my grandson and

I had built together when a sergeant from our police department drove up.

"Mr. Davidson?"

"Yes?"

"Can I talk with you and your wife?"

"What is it?" I asked. "Tell me."

"Mr. Davidson, I regret (rehearsed but said with sensitivity and conviction), I regret to inform you that your son, Aaron, was killed earlier today in a motor vehicle accident."

"No, what, he what?" He gave me a slip of paper with the number for the medical examiner and offered to tell my Lori.

"No, no, seeing a uniform will make it worse; I need to get up there before I fall apart. Thank you," I said, "you are very kind."

As he was walking away, I wanted to chase him down, make him repeat it, make sure I heard him correctly. But I stared at the piece of paper and climbed the stairs.

"No, Andy, no! This can't be happening!" she repeated over and over before collapsing to her knees and then to the floor where she pounded her tears into the hardwood. But she couldn't pound hard enough, and the tears kept coming. "No, no this isn't happening," still echoes in my ears.

But he did die and days later we held our lifeless son in a funeral home before we tried to say goodbye.

When we met with Mr. Domingues, Mr. Koffka, and Mrs. Suman, the head DA said, "Mr. Davidson, we take these matters seriously in Jefferson County, and I can assure you we will get justice, but you will not get satisfaction."

Yet God gave his son. This kept ringing in my ears.

Why my son? I kept asking,

Why?

"Just turn to Jesus," someone said.

"Where was Jesus on the twenty-seventh?" I wanted to cast up.

"Well, you are part of the club," my sister-in-law remarked. I came to realize God was part of the same club; he gave his son, knowing he would die, felt the same emotion, hurt in the same places. When I slipped on the ice carrying my infant son to church during his first winter, I fell, and he was still cradled in my arms. I didn't own him. I was only a steward. God had a different plan for this one.

I can forgive you. I forgive you. After hiking in the rain with tears rolling down my cheeks, I now know where Jesus was on the twenty-seventh. He was there. He lifted my son's soul out of that mire; that one ton of twisted weapon we call a minivan, that bloody carnage, and carried him home.

"Hey, boyz," he [Aaron] would likely say from heaven. "It's kind of a weird world here, in a good way. I can finally pronounce my W's. And now I have tomorrow, T [T was something he and his friends would say. T meant many things but was like Amen]. I'm fine, I'm forgiven, and I forgive you."

"For God so loved the world that he gave his only begotten son that whoever believes in him."

She didn't kill his spirit and she couldn't take his soul. But she did take his life. Idle forever in our farmhouse attic is a pedal tractor, a homemade rocking horse, and a left-handed catcher's mitt waiting for his sons and daughters that will never be. Gone are the countless soccer games and archery lessons he gave to his nephew as a father-figure. Gone. And for that there are consequences. You don't get to choose your punishment; otherwise, it wouldn't be a punishment. You might get to choose your willow switch, but it's up to the Father to decide the punishment, and so that's where we are today.

Thank you for finally pleading guilty; thank you for sparing us one less indignity. You can't take away our pain, but you can add to it. And by delaying and bargaining for a lesser sentence, it did add to the pain. It began when I flew out here for the first hearing. Out of convenience for the defendant's lawyer, the meeting was prearranged the day before with the judge—unbeknownst to me. The pain increased when I flew out here a second time and sat across from an older woman dressed in a pink sweater [the defendant] only to have the pretrial conference delayed. It rarely is delayed more than two times; but it was delayed a third time, not to gather more evidence, but for more time and the defendant continued to drive a two-thousand-pound weapon. We are here for a misdemeanor crime, but we are here because someone died—and someone killed him. So arguing for eleven points on a driver's license rather than twelve points diminished the value of my son to one point and was demeaning to my family. It was in the best interest of the lawyer and not his client.

After dropping her husband off at the golf course and waiting behind other cars, she could have stopped, and could have looked twice. She could have looked for all motorists; be it a car, a motorcycle, or a child on a bicycle, and could have turned right. Instead she crossed three lanes of traffic, chose to disregard the traffic, and overestimated her abilities when she drove in front of my son.

When we met with the DAs in July, we wanted only that the defendant to get up and state, "I did it." That is what Aaron would have done. I have seen him get up and state, "I did it, I am responsible," many times in his brief life. The only thing we asked then and now is that she lose her license for one year. People lose their license for driving too fast, so it was ludicrous to think in this case she should deserve less.

When we met with the head DA in July, he may have gotten it backwards. Whatever you decide today, Your Honor, will fall short of justice. True justice will not occur until we get our son back. But I can say I am satisfied. I am satisfied that Brian, Darren, and Patti worked, used their acumen, and displayed their personal concern for Aaron and for everyone he touched. For that we are grateful and satisfied. On a remote mountain in the Appalachians, I read a solitary tombstone from the early 1900s. It said, 'Not Dead, Just Absent.' It's just as true today.

"For God so loved the world that He gave His only begotten Son, that whoever believes in Him should not perish but have everlasting life"[2].

I sat down and listened to the judge who said he understood how the court can get in the way. He was sympathetic towards the woman who intended no harm and had no history of harm. However, he stated several times that someone who was good was taken from the community and for that a punishment must occur. He sentenced her to ninety days of community service, a one-thousand-dollar court fine, and a one-year loss of license.

As the people filed out of the courtroom, I made my way to her, told her I forgave her, and hugged her. She was motionless, but I could tell she was filled with emotion. At the time, I wasn't aware of my feelings, somewhat like being in a big moment in a game—it's a reaction. Afterward, I felt sympathy for both of us and knew that we were inextricably tied together for the rest of our lives.

Lori was out in the hallway as the group filed past. Aaron's friends surrounded her. She looked calm, but we both knew different. She wanted this day done, because she knew she wouldn't get her what she truly needed.

I returned to our family of boys from Keystone, my daughter, and Lori. We drove to a three-hour lunch. Aaron's ex-girlfriend and her mother joined us. Even though she'd broken up with Aaron, both cared for each other. There were awkward moments, but after Aaron died, everyone got a wide berth.

We talked about Keystone and told stories about Aaron. They laughed about how he would always test the limits, show up in the morning just in time, and make his pot of "level 5" coffee. They recalled one time, he got so frustrated playing ice hockey he illegally hip checked a player only to find out the player was a girl. In time, I may grow to laugh—but on this day, I ached. There was a hole in my heart. I hiked with a hole in my heart.

Death is a novel experience, I wanted to focus on what is truly important and not past details. I didn't want lunch to end because I didn't want to go back to reality. I loved being around those guys listening to them as they told their Aaron stories with us telling some of our own.

I wrote in my journal:

> "...tomorrow morning, I must leave at 0-dark:30. Tomorrow evening, I will be back on the trail, content knowing we did what had to be done. We felt secure from the support and warmth we felt from our friends, secure in our world, and stronger knowing now was our time to walk our walk.
> And walk our walk with God."

I boarded a plane bound for Asheville, North Carolina, where Coma met me.

"Wizard, welcome back."

"Wizard, no more," I told him. "I'm letting the trail pick my name." As we drove to Tennessee, we came upon a dog running along the highway. Coma stopped to pick up the stray and take her to an emergency dog pound to be united with its owner. The old hunting dog's skin draped around her ribs. Her stretched teats swayed as she ran. She was past her prime but still full of life and looking for purpose and a place to call home. She smelled and needed a name. We were alike. Coma didn't know it, but he was part of God's plan helping both of us.

As we drove, I got to tell Coma about the trial and my message. I carried John Eldredge's book, *Wild at Heart*, which describes how men often need to be outdoors to experience the deity of God. John Muir once said he would rather be in the woods thinking about God than in church thinking about being in the woods.

I left my book with Coma. Before he dropped me off, he spotted Miss Janet, the most famous of trail angels. He flagged her down, and I ran up to her van.

"Miss Janet! Miss Janet!" I called like a school kid who just met his idol. I told her how Coma helped me.

In a philosophical manner, she remarked, "The trail has a way of working things out."

I have to write that down. Next to her was Scout, who met up with Miss Janet the day I left for Denver. He was still with her.

After I bought hot dogs for us and the dog, Coma dropped me off at the bridge in front of Uncle Johnny's Hostel. I spent an uneasy night in troll-like fashion under the bridge. I slept without the rain fly to see if anyone approached me. In the morning, I jumped out of my tent and hurried down trail.

"Katahdin [the last mountain in Maine]," I muttered, "Katahdin for Aaron." I walked on, nameless, but renewed. The sun came out, then rain, then hail, and finally, the sun again. I was back in the cycle of the trail.

CHAPTER 7

KILL THE WIZARD

I first thought about hiking the Appalachian Trail after I returned home from Afghanistan at least ten years prior. I'd deployed to a combat zone with Navy SEALs, but I never needed to fire my weapon. If a psychologist gets caught in the middle of a gun battle, something, or someone, has gone terribly awry. I worked with good Americans who risked their lives daily but sometimes did not come home in one piece. I worked with gifted people forced to deal with life when things went wrong. That's when I came in.

Special Operators are on the pointy end of the spear where people can hurt. I helped the men transition home. As the shrink, they sometimes let me into their circle. I ran to the sound of bullets, but I knew they weren't shooting at me. They were shooting at the men I worked with, and after years of hearing their vivid accounts, I felt a part of the team.

On deployment, I thought about backpacking with Lori. The military gave me some cool gear, and I bought more at a North Face outlet in Afghanistan. I wanted to get away after living so closely with other people for several months. Similar to Earl Shaffer, who walked off the war after returning home from World War II, I returned home to hike up Peter's Mountain on the A.T. for three long days.

My heart beat fiercely when Lori and I had started our climb years before in 2005. My pack weighed forty pounds for what I thought would be an easy hike. "Why would anyone want to do this?" I asked myself as I climbed the steep entrance to a whole other world. After a few miles, we set up our tent near a shelter that contained several thru-hikers and trail maintenance workers. I met one worker who talked with fondness about the challenge of a thru-hike.

He planted the notion of thru-hiking the trail in my head. The trail would be a good way to begin a new life after the Navy, I thought. The idea germinated when I hurt my back five years before my hike, and I wrote a list of goals because of the bulging L5 disc in my lower back. At the bottom of the page, I wrote two simple letters—A.T.

The year before my Navy retirement, I planned my trip. I bought books, searched the internet, and found deals on used equipment on a website for ultra-light backpacking. I had talked to Aaron about joining me for part of the trail. As a lift mechanic, he could take vacations in the summer, and he would enjoy the adventure.

Years before, Aaron and I and a friend sailed a small sailboat from Annapolis, Maryland, to Camp Lejeune, North Carolina. The trip took nine days by boat. The distance took nine hours to drive in a car. After I retired from the Navy, I planned on hiking the A.T. If Aaron joined me on the trail, we would fight with each other and make a memory. That all changed on July 27, 2014.

After Aaron died, I moped around the house for months. I needed to do something. My new job became arduous; simple tasks became monumental chores. My thoughts distracted me from any chance of being productive.

I tried to make sense of my world when I built a simple post and beam shed using a hammer, drill, and chisel. Each week, the hour and a half I coached youth soccer provided relief from my thoughts. The thought plagued me that someday a cop might walk up our path again.

Doing nothing drove me mad. I needed a reason to get out of bed in the morning—I needed purpose. When Richard Dreyfus built a huge clay mountain in his living room in the movie *Close Encounters of the Third Kind*, he didn't understand why. The mountain had a gravitational force that pulled him forward. His path took him to Devil's Tower in Wyoming and to a new life. A certain force pulled me to Springer Mountain in Georgia.

I set the date—March thirty-first—when my path would take me toward Mount Katahdin in Maine. Not knowing what I was getting into, just knowing I was doing something, my path got real. I was doing something that mattered.

Now, I was going back to the trail after being in a world of courtrooms and car traffic. Jefferson County made me dizzy. I longed to be back in the quiet, in the simple, in the woods, and Lori needed the salt air, the ocean, and the Outer Banks beach.

I restarted my hike with a renewed sense of optimism and purpose that buoyed my spirit and lifted my feet. The gentle terrain turned favorable when I left Erwin, Tennessee, that morning but soon turned upward. The next day, the path turned into Unaka Mountain standing over five-thousand feet proud.

The onset of sweat took me back to my first trail hike up Cove Mountain in Pennsylvania some thirty-plus years ago. Lori and I joined the Cliber family for a short but steep springtime hike outside Duncannon, our hometown. I remember starting out thinking hiking was easy, but I began sweating and worried if I would make it. That hike was just a walk with friends to the top of Hawk Rock. This hike was a pilgrimage.

I wanted more than a walk. I wanted a life. The life I had was torn asunder by one momentous act, and I wouldn't get my old life back. My first challenge was the sentencing hearing. There would be more. The physical milestone of getting through Georgia didn't compare to the emotional and spiritual battles yet to come. Again, I wondered if I would make it. While off the trail in Colorado I wrote:

> If the trail is going to teach me, I must deal with that control thing that keeps getting in the way. It's laughable how each day I make my plans, and each day the trail changes my plans. Goals are good; a goal without a plan is only a wish or a dream. Wishes and dreams aren't all that bad either, but without some good old-fashioned discipline, little can take place. My problem is that oft the discipline has been the focus. And the focus shifts from God to *moi*.
>
> So I'm moving forward. God said, "So then, because you are lukewarm, and neither cold nor hot, I will vomit you out of My mouth"[3]. Well, I ain't vomit.
>
> I still want to die. WHAT? You heard me. I wanted to die and be with my son. But now "I" want to die. Kill the wizard. "Oh no, I'm a good person, I'm just a bad Wizard." (Wizard of OZ) Well, I was a good Wizard, but I wasn't a good person.
>
> So, bring it, trail. It's time to man up, damn the fear, call me what you will but don't call me forgettable … or vomit.

WHEN SUNDAY SMILED

I was alone on the trail. When I'd meet people for the second time, they never seemed to remember me. By avoiding others, I controlled my world but harbored ill feelings. My pain isolated me. I thought no one understood, no one knew what I felt. Alone, I hiked up the mountain when the weather began raining—then hailed. Hail? Really? Hail?

Because I'd lost someone close, I still wanted to be with him, and I want to be with him now. It's not that I'm suicidal—I know the difference. I will see Aaron again. I pictured him looking at me and saying, "Really? I loved life so much and you took yours?" I couldn't do that to him or my earthly family. But I wouldn't argue if God took me in an accident.

Now instead of dying, I wanted to die to self. I hated dragging around the house in a lukewarm purgatory. I despised not caring. I didn't want to sleepwalk through life. I wanted to thru-hike through life. I had to be all in or all out. I wanted Wizard out and me in. Wizard is what the Marines called me in my old life, but being a Wizard had nothing to do with my life on the trail.

"Okay, God," I prayed, *"I am stepping out in faith."*

I dragged my flickering faith up the rain-soaked hill. The hail was brief, but the rain was persistent. I set up my tent in a quiet spot and settled in before the rain picked up. I didn't get out of my tent when another group of hikers set up camp. They were loud, borderline obnoxious, but they were happy. They had each other. In the morning, I left camp before they ever stirred.

With the temperature dropping, my walking kept me warm and confident. Cold scared me. There are too many stories about experienced hikers succumbing to hypothermia. The disorder will cause a hiker to become disoriented, even delusional, before surrendering to death. I didn't want to be a statistic. I climbed 6,212 feet up Roan Mountain and walked into a snowy section. The flakes looked like crystals laying on the rocks and tree branches. The scene was a Currier and Ives winter picture, so I stopped for lunch.

The only thing I disliked more than cold was hunger—so hunger won out and I made myself a sandwich. The warm sweat inside my clothes turned my layers into a refrigerator. First, I shivered, then my teeth chattered. Before I could finish eating, my hands stopped shaking and froze. The simplest of tasks such as screwing on a lid or zippering a pocket became insurmountable. My stiffened body was slow to move when I got off that rock.

I have to get out of here. Another hiker, Flick from Florida, came bounding up the trail.

"Snow! Cool!" she exclaimed and took pictures. The snow was cool to her, but the weather was co-co-co-cold to me. The white stuff thrilled Flick, who got her name from playing Ultimate Frisbee. I had nothing to fear, but I still hustled down the mountain and away from the mountainous tundra.

I hiked to Over Mountain Shelter, a converted barn where I made my way to the second floor. A group of students from a Christian college were staying the night as part of a wilderness experience. Another thru-hiker asked me what my trail name was, and I told her I didn't have one.

"We have to do something about that," she said.

The next day, I was out of the barn before anyone else got up—and before I had a trail name. The sunny start looked to be a promising day. The wind picked up, and the fog moved in as I started over Little Hump and Hump Mountains with their repeating summits. I met a slight rain which was more of a low, wet fog than real rain, but the wet made for a miserable morning.

As I entered the woods focused on my misery, a section hiker caught up to me, and I picked up my pace. Dave was a Secret Service agent and in great shape. By the time we reached the bottom of the mountain, I forgot how much I hurt and went from misery to mastery in one short day. I went from intense knee pain, wondering if this would be my last day, to an incredible cheeseburger at the bottom of the mountain, and felt an incredible accomplishment at the end of the day, lying in my sleeping bag anticipating the next day to begin. Only a run-on sentence can describe how I felt.

In a few days, I would be in Damascus where Lori and our dog Belle would meet me. Between us were eighty miles. The next day I met another young hiker, Finch, a budding ornithologist from Pennsylvania. We shared a sweet campsite next to a swift stream. Water is an anchor point that draws hikers. The bubbling sounds at night relaxed us and provided a restful sleep.

I took a lot of pictures of water and the bridges over them. They spoke to my inner longing for transition in my life. The endless motion of water evoked wordless emotion that was more than just water and rocks. I found myself alongside water that transcended any earthly misery and inspired me in this world there is peace. There is still a chance I could reach a sense of harmony and a sense of purpose.

Finch was a faster hiker than I was, so the next day despite me leaving first, he overtook me and moved ahead. I stopped at a campsite/hostel to get a short resupply where I ran into Misfit who'd shared a ride with Blurbon and me a month ago in Gatlinburg, Tennessee.

"I've been hiking pretty hard," he told the cashier, "so I think I will zero here." After being off the trail for one week, I caught up with someone I knew from before and realized that I didn't need to worry about my hiking speed. I was hiking just fine.

I hiked past some magnificent falls occupied by a horde of day-hikers. Despite my resupply detour, I managed seventeen miles to Pond Flats, but there was no pond to be found. The site barely had water, but Pond Flats had Finch and two other hikers, Flap Jack and Tunes, who were also from Pennsylvania. Flap Jack made a habit of starting a fire each night and eating pancakes each morning.

We sat around a fire ring joking about Philadelphia sports and the trail while they shared a joint.

"Hey, Andy, do you ... smoke the reefer?" Flap Jack fumbled with his words. Because I was older than his own father, he thought he had to speak a language my generation would understand. I smiled.

"Yesterday, I camped in a rainy spot next to a loud group," I said, "but no one ever saw me before I left the next day."

"You're like a phantom, man," Tunes said after taking a drag. "Hey, Phantom! That's a great trail name."

Phantom, I like it. The next day, I slipped away while Tunes was still in his tent and Flap Jack was frying a pancake.

"See you, Phantom!" Tunes yelled out.

"See you, Tunes!" I smiled. *Phantom beats forgettable any day.* Phantom summed up how I hiked. I trusted the trail, and the trail named me. Part way down the trail, I wrote a small note "Phantom was here," and stuck the paper to a tree hoping that Tunes and Flap Jack would find it. *Phantom, huh?* I smiled at the trees.

I made a policy that every time I saw a white blaze on a tree, I smiled, and every time I saw a double white blaze, I showed teeth. A double white blaze indicated a change in the trail. My policy of smiling kept my attention on the blazes. Smiling helped to lighten my load because when I smiled, I practiced happy. Happiness is a verb. My dour expression pushed people away, so by practicing my smile I learned to greet other hikers. I smiled at the trees but when they didn't smile back, they weren't mad at me—they're trees, that's what trees do.

When I walked into a shelter, the hikers looked down, distracted with their own thoughts. I changed that and made a point of saying hello and smiling until someone responded. I made friends, and we shared vital trail information. My wariness dissipated, and I felt a kinship with my hikers.

I closed in on Damascus, a town famous for its hiker hospitality. Lori made reservations for us at Woodchuck Hostel, and I was eager to meet her there. My system was taking shape. I got up early and started to hike by six or six-thirty. With my new trail name, I talked to others more. The young people I met along the trail accepted me—always polite, always giving. I aimed to do the same.

In route to Damascus, I averaged over twenty miles a day. Walking along the trail, I caught up with a young hiker named Hashtag who told me he lost his father at an early age. His dad was a youth leader, but Hashtag drifted away from the church and into drugs and alcohol. Now he wanted to be a youth leader and get kids involved in the outdoors to help them deal with their fathers and their Father in Heaven.

"I haven't met any other Christians," he stated.

"Well, I met two Christians yesterday—one even had a Bible verse tattooed on her arm, and I met you today." I was opening up to others along the trail and shared my story with Hashtag as we headed down the last descent into town. When he stopped for water, I ran the last few miles alone to town.

Damascus was a strip of stores and businesses nestled between the mountains. The town boasted several hostels. I walked down the street and over the creek to Woodchuck Hostel, owned and operated by Woodchuck, a hiker. Lori drove hours to meet me and got lost in rural Tennessee. The cabin she booked was a converted airy woodshop behind Woodchuck's house. Its rustic décor was as perfect as the waffles in the morning. From our earlier hiking days and just knowing my wife, I knew she could be a rock star on the trail.

Lori brought backpacking meals and my old pack from deployment. Ninety liters, compared to my fifty-five-liter pack, was huge. I freaked out because the pack was just too big. I couldn't convince her to buy a smaller one the next day at the outfitters, so we switched packs and started out of town.

"Hey, Phantom!" yelled Flap Jack from the porch of another hostel, "We got your note!" We ran into Forever and Waiting, a pair of female hikers. Maybe I wasn't forgettable.

"You will be good to get to the first shelter," someone stated. I took the advice as a challenge. I stopped in the middle of the trail to hug Lori and tell her how happy I was to have her and Belle, our dog, of course. Being alone was hard on her. She wouldn't say so, but her expression told otherwise. Now together, I found satisfaction—my wife, our dog, the trail—I had everything I needed.

I must have wanted more because at the first shelter, I decided we could go further. My decision made all the difference. Lori would have been content to stop. Despite being in good shape, she was not in trail shape. Her feet were not used to her boots, and her back was not used to her pack. As we hiked farther, the clouds began to rain. At twelve miles, we stopped along an isolated pond.

Lori was soaked to the core. Her hands were cold, and her positive attitude was waning. I forgot how human she can be, because she is my strength. After setting up the tent, she climbed inside, and I got water to make dinner. I wanted to take care of her. She now sported two huge heel blisters the size of silver dollars. Walking in the rain in new boots on tough terrain proved a bad combination. Instead of being healthy and happy in a dry shelter, we were wet and injured in the middle of the woods.

The next day, I got a good look at her gaping blisters. Despite Second Skin and duct tape, she was in pain. I took most of the pack weight and all of the responsibility. In the military, I learned that good leaders took care of their people. On the trail, I was the leader, but I didn't take care of Lori. My satisfaction from the day prior turned to frustration. Despite all our good feelings, things turned sour. Lori walked quietly behind me. She toughed out twelve more miles where we camped along a road. My attitude was in the toilet, and she was discouraged. Even Belle lagged behind.

Near us, a group of hikers from a halfway house prayed and headed into the woods. Their equipment looked twenty years old. They were clearly out of shape as they finished their last cigarettes to start the hike. *They are so ill-prepared yet so happy.* I envied them and wondered how I could catch their enthusiasm. Enjoy the hike—live in the moment, walk … just walk.

Lori, Belle, and I hiked our third and final day together. On day one, Belle ran through the woods, but now, she laid in the streams to cool off. At night, she laid motionless on our feet in our two-person tent. We planned on hiking much farther, but after three days we were done. I dropped my pack and my frustration poured out of me.

"Why can't I be more like the hikers from the halfway house?" I asked. "Why can't I be happy? Why?" Lori quietly watched my meltdown. She wanted off the mountain.

We hiked in silence and came upon the five-hundred-mile mark. After walking past the trail for Mount Rogers, the highest point in Virginia, we headed into Greyson Highlands, home of the wild ponies. As we walked, a hiker approached us and gave us a pair of wooden crosses with "Love" inscribed on mine and "Faith" inscribed on Lori's.

We met a trail maintenance team at the Scales, a place that used to corral livestock. I told our story to a volunteer, of beginning in Damascus and ending with two huge blisters.

"Do you need more water?" George asked.

"We really need a ride to town," I replied.

"I'm going to Damascus and am coming back tomorrow," he stated.

Talk about trail magic. Broken, we needed help, and George was our trail angel. If God takes care of the birds of the air, then surely he cares more for Lori and me. We climbed into that old man's Chevy S10 and made our way down a difficult dirt road that used to support a narrow-gauge railroad.

After getting Lori's car in Damascus, we found a restaurant and a clean motel in Abington. That night, I woke her up to talk. I tried to convince her to take time off and come back out, but her blisters convinced her to go home.

"I'm fine," she said, "I got out on the trail, I got to see what it's like, and I found out it's tougher than I thought." She told me not to worry. Typical. She was thinking of me. But I felt awful. I was guilty and apologized profusely.

Our trail angel picked me up the next morning. I was pathetic. I left my wife behind and I wanted a "do over." I missed the opportunity to show her the trail I that I loved. But because of a series of decisions, from equipment to hiking to attitude, I blew it. I didn't rise above the circumstances—I just blew it.

Along the trail, I met people who, despite the circumstances, were always positive, always encouraging. They were magnetic—other hikers were drawn to them. They were special, and I wanted to be them on and off the trail. The Bible talks about Barnabas whose name even means encouragement. I wanted to be Barnabas.

George and I drove back up that mountain when he told me he lost his twenty-four-year-old son thirty years ago. His son would have been around my age. I told him I lost my son last year. We drove in silence, quiet tears rolling down my face. In the quiet, I felt close to George. After I walked away, I shouted back from fifty yards and waved as I attempted to show how much his kindness meant. That man knew.

God had a plan. George was my Barnabas. God took care of us. I focused on my worries and did not recognize his plan until it was too late.

For the next many miles, I walked with tear-stained eyes as I cried aloud to God. "Make me a man." John Eldridge's book *Wild at Heart* states that wives look to their husbands for strength. I was not strong. I looked to my wife for strength. She needed me strong.

"Make me a man," I repeated. "Make me strong," I said as I walked up on a group of hikers.

Young Blood and four others sat behind a van enjoying beer and soda. I'd met Young Blood back in Georgia where we shared our military stories about SERE: Search, Evasion, Resistance, and Escape School. SERE is two weeks of survival training including several days of captivity. Young Blood was real, unlike many of the military poseurs I met along the way—people who wore their old gear and talked about the glory days. Young Blood wore no Army gear but spoke with authenticity. He caught up to me, because he knew I was hurting. That evening was his last night on the trail, but he let me talk about my hike with Lori. He was another hiker who drifted in and out of my life along the trail and ministered in so many ways.

Completing a thru-hike is a defining moment of humility, not a feat of pride. I could not do this alone. Young Blood was struggling with the prospect of a new job that would pull him from the trail. He enjoyed the culture of the trail and the solitude of the woods but had decided to work with youth in an Outward-Bound program.

"Remember, hike your own hike," Young Blood implored as he left the trail at Friendship Shelter near Marion, Virginia the next day.

At the crossroads of Atkins, I was told there was a Dollar General a mile down the road. Over two miles later, I asked a motorist for a ride, and he drove me two additional miles. He wore the Confederate stars and bars on his hat but listened to rap music on the radio. I found out he was from Detroit and liked Eminem. Grace is bigger than judgment.

After getting back to the trail, I settled into a tick-infested field next to the sounds of a busy highway. Today was Mother's Day, and Lori was alone. I called her on a sketchy connection. I knew how tough this day was on her. We knew Aaron would have called today. She looked forward so much to hearing her children's voices. We knew Ali and Robby would call, but just like the shepherd who left his sheep for one that was lost, we grieved for our lost one. Aaron isn't lost; he is the one found, but the loss still hurts. That pain magnifies on anniversaries and holidays. And on Sundays, the day he died. Sundays hurt.

Century-old farms and meadows flank Virginia's mountains. Its trails are well-maintained due to the Potomac Area Trail Club. The state is blessed with people who care about the trail and a trail that covers a reasonable terrain.

Flask stood next to an innocuous sign. "Pretty cool sign, huh?" he asked. The four by eight piece of wood screwed to a tree marked the one-quarter point of the trail.

"Wow, I almost walked right past it," I confessed. I had walked one-quarter of the Appalachian Trail. I wanted to get to the 1,000-mile mark and get through Virginia. I'd heard Virginia was easy. I'd heard wrong. I was still looking for easy. The following is from my journal:

> I meet so many happy people along the way, it's bewildering.
> I'm not trying to punish myself out here, but that's what I
> am doing. I've slowed my pace, I stop and take pictures, and

sometimes, I even stop just to touch the texture of the trees. I am mystified watching how others bond out here. "What's your trail name" and "How far did you hike today?" seem to be the best conversation starters. After that I got nothing—and drift back to my tent or walk down to the water to wash my socks. I know I am missing out, but I'm tired and have little to give. I want to be part of the culture, but so far, I'm more of an observer/participant.

I hiked on, looking for the way to Katahdin and a better way to God and man.

CHAPTER 8

Trail Days

I grew trail legs after walking twenty miles and more on most days. My quads grew stronger, but I pushed myself too hard. I dismissed my fatigue when I passed the six-hundred-mile marker, took a picture, and walked away.

Earlier hikers marked the trail. Each hundred-mile point was marked by rocks that spelled out the number. I looked forward to these marks as they brought a sense of accomplishment and subsequent pride. A new state was always satisfying, but real progress is measured in miles. My hike took forever to get to one hundred miles; now my sights were set on a thousand miles. As I walked, I crunched numbers to figure out one-eighth, one-fifth, one-quarter of the trail, and so on.

I calculated mileage to keep me motivated, but my real motivation was my family, friends, and God. The beauty that surrounded me daily provided more than a distraction. Before I left, Lori reminded me of the beautiful sites I would encounter. "Oh, yeah," I said. Lori loves growing and arranging flowers. I never gave them much thought. She grows flowers in our front yard and arranges them for church. Sometimes, she asks me if I noticed them. Sometimes I did. She stops for turtles and butterflies. I stop when I'm tired.

When I started this hike, the destination meant everything, and the journey was an obstacle. Now, the sights and smells of the woods enveloped me. The journey became my purpose.

I didn't need mathematical equations to keep me entertained, and I didn't need music. Sometimes, I made up my own songs and sang like David in the book of Psalms. I pictured the future king as a shepherd protecting his flock from wild animals. To pass the time, he sang songs to his Lord. Sometimes I enjoyed the quiet. I didn't need distractions—I had the woods.

When I first established a blog, I intended to keep my unfiltered rants to myself. I found that the people reading my blog became a source of motivation. Every day quitting entered my mind. I pictured my last blog entry, *"I quit."* Well, I couldn't quit the people supporting me or myself.

I also couldn't tell my grandson Jayden that I quit. I imagined sitting on a soggy log next to my ten-year-old man with an oversized poncho holding on to a cold cup of cocoa. He'd look up at me with his trusting eyes, believing I would take care of him. He believed in me, and I would not violate that trust.

I pictured telling him, "I quit." He would look up at me, give me a hug, and be glad I came home. He is that kind of kid. I should have a bracelet that reads "WWJD." Not "What Would Jesus Do?" but rather, "What Would Jayden Do?" When Jayden was small enough to be in a car seat, I stopped at a red light and expressed my disgust we missed the light.

He looked up and exclaimed, "We're first!" That's perspective. Back home in Colorado, he followed me on a map of the Appalachian Trail. He was my primary earthly motivation; I could not disappoint.

The trail is in constant flux due to repairs to the worn-out sections. The Appalachian Trail Conservancy continues to secure land to assure the trail continues to have a home. In the past, the trail traversed miles of road and private land. Today, almost the entire trail is on mountainous land—difficult mountainous land. The trail has become a trough due to erosion from water and foot traffic. Mountain topsoil is thin; even a small amount of hiking will disturb the fragile ecosystem.

This year, the trail grew four miles due to adding more switchbacks to help the ecosystem heal. The trail's ups and downs are an easy target for complaints, but these elevations make the A.T. Other trails, such as the Pacific Coast Trail and the Continental Divide Trail, part of the Triple Crown of thru-hiking, have more mild grades. The PCT uses pack animals to improve their trails. The abundance of trees on the Appalachian Trail, matched with the abundance of rain, exposed rocks, and roots made for a tough outing. The trail is rarely a broad path through the woods. The path is just a few feet wide sheltered with trees that grow over the walkway to create a green canopy. The trail is tough.

On the trail and in life, some people love to complain about everything they cannot control. They focus on the rocks and ignore their resolve.

Life is tough and doesn't get any easier. Some days, I hiked over twenty miles, some days only twelve. Regardless of the miles, every day challenged me. My choice whether I focused on the trail or on me was on me. My choice to focus on my wet feet or my dry sleeping bag—on me. Whether I focused on being stuck at a red light or first in line was, again, all my choice. God has a plan for my life, but I have a choice in how I deal with that plan.

Southern Virginia proved to be just as tough as Tennessee. As I hiked alone, I continued to meet fellow hikers along the way. Rougarou and Palomino, a couple from Louisiana, had a childlike enthusiasm for the trail. A Rougarou is a mythical werewolf that roams the bayou, and a palomino is a specially colored horse. They told me they stayed by the river because they had so much fun building rock sculptures, stacking rocks on top of each other. They didn't know the sculptures went against the "leave no trace" philosophy of the trail. Rules didn't seem to slow them down.

On top of a grassy clearing, Michael Angelo, who I had not seen since Georgia, was kneeling in a meadow off the trail. He beckoned to me to where a vulnerable fawn lay in the grass. The newborn deer looked so innocent. We figured its mother was not far and might be watching us. Looking at its white spots and round dark eyes brought on a sense of purity. In a harsh world, there is still gentleness—we just have to look for it. Sometimes it's right beside us, lying in the weeds. We left the little guy undisturbed after taking a quick picture.

I finished walking twenty-six miles and made my way to a private campsite next to Trent's Grocery General Store. After eating with other hikers, I stayed at the campsite where I got a shower, did my laundry, and sat by the campfire. Michael Angelo, Dirty Bird, Rougarou, Palomino, and Captain K, the curious airplane pilot, sat around the fire. Captain K was a hospital administrator who had a pilot's license. He broke into people's conversations and had a quirky take on the world. Captain K ran around the campsite looking for something to burn in the fire. The broken-down campsite was transformed as we laughed and joked into the night. The next day we left camp at different times to hike our own hikes.

I found Michael Angelo's prized feather in the middle of the trail, hoping I would catch up to him, but I never did, and the feather fell out of my pack. Later, I found out that Michael Angelo had taken a spur trail to a waterfall, so when he returned to the trail, he was behind me and found his feather sitting on the trail. Even when we fail to deliver, God has a plan.

Two hundred miles back in Damascus, the town was preparing for the biggest Trail Days on the A.T. Hikers from all along the trail were making their way back for the hiker festival. Trail Days sounded like fun. The event didn't sound like me, but I was changing. I was acculturating to the trail community and the Damascus Trail Days was the hiker event of the year.

The A.T. is not a solitary pursuit; but a community. It's a unique culture complete with trail names, angels, and magic, unlike any other trail. Just like the vistas and views, the community was something I did not expect but was just what I needed. I didn't know what Jayden would do in this situation, but I knew Aaron would go to Trail Days. He always had time for friends or family. "Today is all we have, 'T,'" he told his coworkers, now inscribed on a plaque posted at his ski mountain. "T" was slang which has no specific translation but is the equivalent of "amen," or "yeah, man."

Today, I walked into Pearisburg. Like so many trail towns, Pearisburg had a well-established downtown but was left with more abandoned buildings than businesses. Its beautiful buildings evidenced a once-thriving manufacturing economy. Now manufacturing has moved on and left Pearisburg in its wake.

As I strolled down the street that morning, I had a curious new attitude—I felt blessed. My feeling was more than the sum of walking into town and thinking about a real meal. I am blessed with good health, good family, and good friends, but rarely have I allowed myself the benefit of my blessings. Today was different—I woke-up blessed.

I called Lori, choked up and told her, "I'm blessed, Lori, I'm blessed, I can't explain it, we'll talk later." Lori prayed for my attitude, but I surprised her so early in the morning. I didn't tell her about going to Trail Days. I still felt blessed when two guys and a girl came out of a building near the center of town.

"Hey, do you know where the restaurant is?" I asked.

"No," came the terse reply, which should have been a clue, but remember, I'm blessed.

"What I really need is a ride to Damascus," I continued.

"Where's that?"

"Near Abington."

"We're going to Wytheville, that's near Abington," his brother responded. "We could take you there for forty bucks."

"How about twenty," I bargained.

"How about twenty, a pack of Marlboro Reds, and a can of Skoal," came the quick counter.

I didn't know how much a pack of Reds or a can of Skoal cost, but the deal sounded good to me. I got in the backseat of their aging Chevy with the leader sitting next to me, his brother and the girl sat up front.

"So, what's in Wytheville?"

"I have to pick up my wife. She's getting out of jail today."

Jail? Did he just say jail? The pokey, the slammer, the big house? Did he say jail? Visions of abducted hikers and dismemberment normally would have flooded my consciousness, but remember, I was blessed. He was eating mini sausages out of a can at 9:30 in the morning. I was riding with three strangers in a car on an unfamiliar road and couldn't get cell phone reception. I was on my way to the county jail, and I wasn't worried—I felt blessed.

But when he threw the empty can out the window without a second thought, I lost my breath for a moment. *You're that guy, I always wanted to meet you. You're that guy who has been trashing my roads.* He may as well have kicked a dog when he threw that can out the window. *Could he throw me out the window?*

We drove on.

I had to ask, "So what's she in for?" You are never supposed to ask what they are in for, but I couldn't contain myself.

"I wrote some bad checks," the litterer said as he looked at me with a mixture of embarrassment and just a twinge of guilt.

Wait, you wrote the checks, and she is doing the time. Why? Is it because you have priors and if you got arrested, you would do some serious time? And if you have priors, what are they?

While wondering if he really had kicked a dog, he turned and stated, "Don't worry man, we're not going to do anything funny."

63

Oh my gosh, he is reading my mind. He really has kicked a dog!

When I got cell phone reception, I typed in Wytheville into my cell phone. Wytheville was nowhere near Abington. The town was over an hour away. I exclaimed my dismay, and the two brothers began to point fingers due to their geographical blunder. I haggled with them for twenty dollars more if they would drive me the extra hour and a half. The driver wanted to help me, but he had to get his mother's car home when she got out of work. He needed the twenty dollars, but he had a pressure washing job waiting for him later in the day.

When we got to the jail, the wife apparently had a late check-out. The girl in the front seat turned around and told me that she and the driver got married last week. *You just got married and you are spending your honeymoon picking up your sister-in-law at the county jail?* She started to make fun of the prisoners as they were doing some landscaping outside the fence.

"Yeah, boys, work hard," she taunted under her breath.

Please don't upset the inmates.

The brothers decided to take me to the local truck stop where I would try to get a ride down I-81 to Damascus.

"Look at this face," I said, "This is not a face that gets rides at a truck stop." I wasn't optimistic about getting a ride based on my earlier hitchhiking record, but I did something different this time—I trusted God.

The husband waited for his wife at the jail, and the newlyweds took me to the truck stop. I was relieved not to be there when his wife got released thinking the reunion would not be pleasant. I assumed she would be just a little upset knowing that she spent a week in the slammer for something her husband did.

At the truck stop, I had other concerns. I needed a ride. I stood near the truckers' entrance and asked drivers for a ride.

"No, I can't take passengers, company policy, you need an owner operator," came the repeated responses. One trucker asked me where I was headed.

"Damascus."

"Where's that?"

"Near Abington."

"Where's that?"

"Down I-81."

"You got to get an owner/operator."

"Then why did you ask me about Damascus?" I exclaimed. "That's like the driver who waved at me the other day when I hitchhiked. Waving did nothing for me."

The trucker shrank away, surprised by my irritation. I needed a new tactic before I got kicked out of the truck stop. I reached a new low when I moved in front of the men's room and solicited for a ride. Men dried their hands and looked over their shoulders as they walked away from me shaking their heads no. I noticed one traveler who wore a retired Navy ball cap.

"Hey, shipmate," I called out, and he turned with a big smile.

"I know it's a total manipulation on my part, but I'm hiking the Appalachian Trail and I'm trying to get to Damascus," I stated.

"Where's that?"

"Near Abington."

"Where's that?"

"Down I-81," I replied, again wondering if the conversation and I were going anywhere.

We looked at an atlas in the store and found that Damascus was on his way. This fine trail angel agreed to drop me along the highway. I bought Tom a cup of coffee and we got back on the road. Tom, a retired Senior Chief with twenty-six years, and me, a retired Captain with twenty years, shared sea stories while en route. He retired in 1992, the year I entered the military, so our careers spanned over forty-six years of history and all the enlisted and officer ranks except Master Chief and admiral. Tom agreed to get off the highway and drop me off in town. He even gave me his number and told me he could pick me up when he returned north on Sunday. By the time he left, I'd made a friend. I really am blessed.

Getting to Trail Days was the best part of being there. My trail angels—the kids in the car and Tom—were good people. They were trying to get by in life and helped a stranger along the way. They were part of God's plan for me.

I arrived at Trail Days on Friday afternoon and returned to Woodchuck Hostel where Lori and I had spent a night. Woodchuck allowed me to pitch my tent along with about thirty other tents in his back yard. Over a thousand other hikers stayed at the tent city on the edge of town. A bonfire burned all night in tent city and hikers regressed into a primordial existence as they danced to the beat of tribal drums. The stories get exaggerated over time, but Woodchuck Hostel was close enough to tent city for me.

Trail Days attracts vendors selling outdoor gear, clothes, art, and food. The town has entertainment throughout the day. Hikers from years past return for a reunion, and many of this year's hikers regard Trail Days as an end to itself. Some men crossdressed or found other ways to stand out. I saw many friends I made along the trail. A mother/daughter team I met during my first week on the trail told me about my old partner Just Greg, who was several hundred miles ahead. They encouraged me to reconnect with him.

The trail is a little like high school as hikers have a newfound youth and optimism. Relationships begin and break up in a matter of days. If the trail  is like high school, then Trail Days is commencement. Commencement marks the beginning of one's life, not the end of school or the trail. Trail Days comes complete with a printed yearbook and a prom. They even elect a prom king and queen.

"I could be prom king," I told Lori on the phone.

"I can't believe you went to Trail Days." She repeated, "I can't believe you went to Trail Days."

I was having fun, and she laughed to hear about it. The height of the festivities was the hiker parade. Making hikers hike a mile down main street seemed a little ironic, and soaking them with water pistols, a little sadistic. But I hiked and I laughed with my friends.

I got a Trail Days' deal on a new pack and a pair of hiking shoes. My old pack had no suspension and weighed heavily on my shoulders. My new pack was light, rested on my hips and floated on my back. My pack was twenty percent off, and my shoes were fifty percent off. The savings paid for my trip and the can of Skoal. I guess I am blessed.

It began to rain the next day. I called my trail angel Tom, who told me he'd left his event early. That worked fine for me due to the downpour. I watched and listened to the music at the edge of the festivities. Vendors lined the narrow park trying to sell cotton candy, tie-dyed dresses, and hammocks.

Tom picked me up, and we drove past Wytheville for another hour to Pearisburg. The trip ended at about 10:00 at night, so I booked a room at the local hotel. The next day, Tom took me to breakfast, to Walmart, and to the trailhead. Yes, I am blessed.

As I headed north with a smile on my face, I had a story. My story had drama, humor, and my story had meaning. I was getting out of my shell. Maybe I am an extrovert. When I stopped at a cemetery and ended up going the wrong way, I shrugged and went on. I had to backtrack at least a mile. When I realized what I had done, I found trail magic hanging in a bag on a tree. A pack of Second Skin for blisters was in it, which I would need in the future.

My new shoes fit well, but new shoes can bring trouble. My feet got wet quicker, and I also slipped more. As the sun went down, I got off the trail to look for a spot to camp along a small creek. My feet got tangled in the thick vines, landing me in the shallow water. My elbow smacked against a flat rock.

That's gonna leave a mark. I winced as I got to my feet. My fall didn't leave a mark but my elbow bothered me for the rest of the hike. I gathered myself and looked at my bent Walmart pole and stuffed it into a side pocket on my pack.

Using hiking poles didn't seem necessary when I first started the trail, but I bought a pair back in Franklin, Tennessee. They propelled me going uphill, they helped me brake going downhill, and they helped me set a pace on the flat. Poles provided the balance to carry the thirty pounds on my back.

Falling provided perspective. A hike can end on one fall. Falling is humbling. I got angry and disheartened. As a youth, football, soccer, and wrestling taught me how to take a fall. Every time, I got up and kept walking after I did a quick body assessment. Not until New England did I learn to put my trust in God, moment by moment.

It takes a certain amount of athleticism to stay healthy on the trail: hiking is not just walking; it's hiking. But athleticism will take you only so far. As time wore on, I realized God's hand in my daily life. I still fell, but God watched over every step I took. I felt his hand on my back. The big miles I logged tired me. When I fell I knew I needed to stop for the night. I set up my tent by flashlight in the stealthiest of sites. The tight fit between the low hanging branches suited my style.

WHEN SUNDAY SMILED

I lost over twenty pounds from the start of my hike. The lack of protein and calories contributed to my lethargy. The precarious balance between carrying calorie-laden food and packing light was the difference between walking tired or going to bed hungry. My daily menu started with two packets of oatmeal, hot chocolate, and a Pop-Tart chaser. A protein bar kept me going until lunch. That's when I broke out the salami, cheese, and peanut butter sandwiches. A Clif Bar around 4:00 kept me on my feet until I found a place to camp.

I carried two liters of water and stopped once, maybe twice a day to refill at a stream. I disliked filtering water. Okay, I hated filtering water. Filtering called for patience when I was thirsty, hungry, and tired but had to be done.

For dinner, I boiled some variation of noodles or rice, threw in some tuna, and garnished it with crackers, elevating the concoction to casserole status. An occasional moon pie sufficed for dessert. I never tired of my menu and looked forward to dinner each day. I thought about that moon pie in my backpack while I hiked. Fifty-cent's worth of junk food motivated me.

The next day, the weather continued to rain, the trail continued to have slippery rocks, and I continued to walk for twenty miles. The ridge lines tested me, the views were awesome, and the farms in the Virginian valleys made me homesick for Pennsylvania. More miles lay between me and my home state. I didn't know the East had a continental divide, but now that I did, I left the geological wonder behind. My Trail Days experience was a high point of my hike. Highs and lows came daily and sometimes covered multiple days. Daleville lay ahead, while multiple days tested my commitment.

CHAPTER 9

WAITING ON GOD

I grew comfortable hiking alone and even more comfortable meeting and making new friends along the way. *I am part of the trail.* Then I came upon a rattlesnake ten feet from the trail. Its rattle alerted me and gave me something new to worry about. Like Indiana Jones said, "Snakes, I hate snakes."

I hiked into the evening to a memorial dedicated to Audie Murphy. The stone rested on the summit of Brush Mountain, within my grasp. A younger hiker walked behind me, so out of foolish pride I pushed hard to lead the way. *If Audie Murphy was awarded three Purple Hearts to become the most decorated service member, then I can get to his memorial before dark.* As the sun faded in the background, I sat in front of a granite slab sweating and thanking Sergeant Murphy for his sacrifice to his country. I prayed I would take care of my family with equal conviction.

The next day, I almost missed Dragon's Tooth. I hesitated to go the quarter mile off the trail until another hiker told me about how impressive the massive bolders looked. The site was an amazing rock formation that jutted out of the ground on an angle that looked like a dragon's tooth. The rocks pointed over twenty feet towards the sky. Hikers climbed up and around them. The formation was big enough that I could find a private place to lay down on the warm stone until I left. I struggled to hike a quarter mile uphill in the hot sun to the trail ridge. Shortly, I came upon another series of small stones that spelled out "700." Surpassing the seven-hundred-mile mark meant I'd finished one-third of the trail, but I wasn't excited.

The doldrums of Virginia were upon me. Not that Virginia is hard, but the flatter state isn't easy, either. By this point, hikers are stronger and can put in more miles. But these miles come at a cost. As I was closing in on the half-way point, my body told me something, but I didn't listen.

In my blog, I recorded:

> Oh, yeah, another milestone of my own. I crossed the 700-mile mark. Almost 1/3 of the trail under my belt, yet every day remains a challenge to both body and spirit. I try to stay motivated by thinking about others suffering from serious illness. If they can endure the rigors of chemo and the prospect of death, then I can endure a little fatigue and pain surrounded by God's handiwork in bloom.

When Aaron died, I thought of nothing other than my grief. I tried to be empathetic to others, but my grief consumed me. I had little room for others' suffering. If I met someone who lost a child, they were part of my club—but everyone else was an outsider. As I hiked, my selfish perspective melted away like the snowflakes on Roan Mountain. Before Aaron died, I considered dedicating my hike to my friend Bob, who died of cancer. I have several friends who are battling this wretched disease, and I investigated raising money. After the accident, I considered no one but me. Now, I had time to pray for everyone in my life. I had time to pray for my enemies and my friends. Okay, I had more time for my friends.

Robert, a friend and associate pastor, was right, I was closer to God's ear. Tony, one of my best friends, had a son battling lymphoma. Younger than Aaron, he began a promising career in the music industry before his diagnosis. My friend Jeff eventually lost his battle with prostate cancer while other friends, Josie and Alison, endured their chemotherapy while I hiked the trail. I prayed for them all.

Then there was Bob, who'd had a lung transplant only to develop an aggressive cancer. I rode my motorcycle to meet him in Clearwater, Florida, where we took in the Phillies spring training. We were going to ride to Bike Week in Daytona when he relapsed. He entered the hospital and never came out. Bob left behind his wife and two broken-hearted daughters. Cancer sucks.

But I'm alive and I can walk. I lost a son; yet, I am blessed. With daily tears in my eyes, I reached out to God and to others. It really doesn't matter whose pain is greater. Pain is pain. Within it, there is something noble and something cursed, but pain still hurts. After all, it's pain.

I was about to experience my own pain in Daleville, but before I did, I hiked to McAfee's Knob, the most photographed point along the trail. I met up with Papa Al and Glamper. Glamper got his name for his glamorous style of camping. Papa Al, much Glamper's senior, joked that he hadn't seen his tent in weeks because Glamper made reservations at the best hostels. Glamper took care of his senior partner. As much as I liked being around this duo, our hiking styles never matched up, so I hiked on my way again.

As I headed toward town, I stopped for lunch at a shelter and looked at the log book. My cold fingers struggled to make a peanut butter sandwich. *It's way too cold for May.* After working up a sweat, I shivered in the shadow of the shelter. I asked Giggles, who I hadn't seen since the Smokies, to help me zipper my pack because my fingers stopped working. Will and Way (where there's a Will there is Way), a couple who would soon celebrate their fiftieth wedding anniversary, remarked that our shelter meeting sounded like we were having a party.

In hindsight, stopping at this shelter may have led to my demise in Daleville, but meeting Will and Way saved me. They told me about staying at the Howard Johnson's Motel for forty dollars. I often avoided the expense of hotels, but getting a room by myself sounded enticing. When they told me about the all-you-can-eat breakfast, I was convinced to get a room key.

My discounted room included cracked bathroom tiles, peeling wallpaper, and stained carpets. But the dated TV got most of the cable channels, and my bed was soft. I resupplied at the supermarket and bought new hiking poles at the outfitters before heading to a pizza parlor.

Sitting down with Glamper and Papa Al at the pizza parlor, I ordered a designer pizza with pretzel crust and basil leaves. Never again. I spent the rest of the night surrounded by cracked porcelain. I was never so sick in all my life. I hurled like a remake of *The Exorcist*. The eight feet to the bathroom almost proved to be eight feet too far.

In the morning, I did something a Davidson never does—I missed the included all-you-can-eat breakfast. The only thing worse than getting a hotel without a free breakfast is missing said breakfast. My Scottish roots would deem this unconscionable.

The next day, I walked two blocks to an urgent care. Twelve other hikers came down with the same symptoms in the same area. "Norovirus," the doc told me, "not designer pizza." Norovirus is a collection of viruses first diagnosed in Norwich, Ohio, in 1972. The virus transmits through contaminated food and water. Noro is a hardy virus, which can survive on other surfaces including paper, pens, and wood surfaces. Several trail blogs mentioned the prominence of this nasty germ in the Daleville area. Being tired, deficient, and susceptible, I walked right into the perfect viral storm.

Hygiene in the woods is lacking. Also, the high miles clearly wore down my immunity. I put in too many miles; I was tired. I may have picked up the virus at the last shelter before town. Regardless what the doctor told me, I would not eat pizza for a long time. *Basil leaves on pizza?* What was I thinking?

The hiker next door had the virus while his brother, who shared everything with him, went untouched. The virus had the resemblance of the Passover or a medieval plague, but not quite the same proportions. I stayed in my room for three days surrounded by falling wallpaper and stained carpet.

I watched TV and ate nothing more than a Wendy's chicken sandwich. My weight plummeted into the 140s as I drained most of the water from my system. If my condition continued, I would have to go home to recuperate.

I recorded in my journal:

> After a Wendy's chicken sandwich and Coke, I thought I would get back on the trail the next day. Tonight will be the third night at a tired motel in Daleville, VA, and I don't know when it will end. Never wanting to do one zero, I did three zeroes. I've been putting in too many miles, stressing this old body, living in the wild, lacking hygiene, and thinking I could rise above the obvious. I need to pray, to listen to God, and wait on him. I don't even like waiting at Wendy's.

After three nights, I had to do something. I planned hiking two miles to the Troutville town park where the fire station had laundry and the park had a bathroom. *Two miles?* I needed to start slow. And I needed a real bathroom before heading into the woods. The park proved to have an added blessing.

A young couple walked into the park carrying all their food in a five-gallon pail. The guy had picked up two cans of dog food while dumpster diving but didn't have a dog. I suggested that he give the cans to a church group that was picnicking at the park, but I demanded he had to bring back dessert.

"Don't bring back a hot dog," I insisted as he walked toward the group, "Dessert."

"It worked," he exclaimed. "They invited us for dinner." The church got dog food, and we got fed. Several hikers, and even some bicyclists, joined the picnic. The bikers were riding the Transamerica Bike Trail that crosses the country from Washington, DC, to Washington State.

"Wait a second," I joked, "You mean biking only takes you three months, you get to stay in towns, and you don't have to filter your water? You even coast on the downhills and you get to sit down all day." Biking sounded like a great idea.

After we ate, one woman handed out some religious tracts.

"Humph, the pamphlet says the Bible is a fact," remarked one hiker.

I didn't know what to say. I didn't know how to talk to someone who had no foundation. The dynamic repeated several times along the trail. I got better as more opportunities came up, but I struggled with talking about my faith to complete strangers. I needed a story.

The next day, I said goodbye to the park and indoor plumbing and stepped into the wild. Still feeling the effects of Norovirus, I exercised restraint. Stopping after only twelve miles seemed strange. After a good night's rest, I left late, walked leisurely, and stopped at a reasonable time after seventeen miles. I escaped a demon and was back in the safety of the woods. The mileage no longer concerned me.

After coming so close to leaving the trail, I reflected on what I had learned. Thru-hiking through life means that I want to take what I learn on the trail and apply the lessons to my daily life. I want to live like I hike. In my journal, I wrote thru-hiking through life means:

> Just walk.
> Leave a small footprint.
> HYOH, hike your own hike.

When your mood turns sour, look up, and realize you are likely climbing.

Stay positive on the uphill and don't worry when the downhill is tougher than the uphill.

No regrets, none.

Smile at the trees. They don't hate you when they don't smile back.

Uphill is good for the heart, downhill is bad for the knees

Let it go, man, Let … It … Go

Just walk.

I expect my list will grow.

Or maybe my list will get shorter.

My list is summed up with the mantra, "Just Walk." Just walk means if I am going to do anything, I must do something. I must get moving. So often, I get caught up in "analysis paralysis," afraid to move until I have all the answers. Life doesn't provide all the answers. I have to step out in faith and walk. Jesus said, "Take up your cross and follow me."[4] Just walk.

Life is simple. Simple does not mean easy. Life is difficult—simple but difficult. We make life complex. My psychology profession built an industry out of complex. Sometimes making issues complex gives us time to sort out the questions when we really don't know what to ask. Finding the right question can be complex. "Why did my son die?" is complex. "How am I going to live?" is a better question. Psychology can help frame the question but falls short on most answers.

When I ask the "Why?" question, I'm at my worst. Why is an easy question to ask because there is no answer. Rather than talk about something I can change, like myself, I project blame on my environment. Sometimes it's the weather, the trail, God, or all three.

My son was dead. When I wanted to quit, I couldn't sit down in the middle of the trail because no one would pick me up and carry me to bed. Despite losing twenty pounds, I was still too big for that. I needed to keep going, but where would I go? That is where the trail helped. I walked the white blazes.

God's world opened when everything I needed was on my back and my only concern was the next blaze. Meeting Just Greg, Coma, or Tom was not a coincidence. And losing the small plastic piece off the bottom of my hiking pole, and three days later a stranger gave me the exact piece wasn't a coincidence. People on the trail and people who knew nothing about the trail provided for me. Ending up in a motel room retching was part of a plan. God was working in my life.

God worked in my life off the trail, but my life was too cluttered for me to grasp his hand. I cluttered my life with details, deadlines, and stuff I didn't need.

I thought I cluttered my life with grief—but I had life backwards. Grief can't be avoided. Grief showed me how cluttered my life had become. With the death of my son, I realized that life mattered and nothing else. Life didn't care that he broke his curfew as a kid. Life didn't care that he didn't go to a four-year college program. Life mattered. That's it. Everything else is vanity.

I cluttered my life with career, promotion, and status. That stuff just made me look good. I cluttered life with appearance. Death didn't care that I was a Navy Captain. Death didn't care that I was a shrink. Death didn't care that I was a Christian, either. When Aaron died, nothing else mattered.

Aaron told me, "Dad, don't worry about me; I'm a Christian. I stand up for what I believe at work. I know I don't do everything I should." His boss and surrogate father, Grant, said that Aaron lived by a code. He was a cowboy who committed to everything in his life; to his work and his play. That matters; that kept me walking.

And walk is what I did. That night, I met up with Waiting who was forever waiting for her partner, Forever. I guess she tired of waiting and the pair split up. Now she sat with her boyfriend, who joined her for a week along with Cruise Control, Mr. Clean, and a group of section hikers around a camp fire.

A couple gave me the rest of their chocolate pudding they'd mixed in a bag. As I dug into it, I turned the bag inside out and licked the chocolate off the plastic. The pudding tasted so good. I was thoroughly immersed until I looked up and noticed everyone staring at me like I was an anteater sifting out the last ant in a rotten log. I had chocolate all over me. After licking the last remnants off my fingers, I excused myself to the spring to get some water and some distance.

The next day, I caught up to Waiting and her boyfriend at the James River suspension bridge. They told me about the trail challenge of jumping off the thirty-foot-high suspension bridge. I've jumped off other heights when I was much younger, and I remembered how different the world looks when you are thirty feet in the air. And the difference scared me. I was afraid I'd hit my head on the bridge and fall to a watery death. The only challenge I needed was Katahdin, but when Waiting and her Special Forces boyfriend jumped, I jumped. I felt a force pushing me back to the safe bridge, but I pushed harder. Or maybe I let go. Either way, a sense of freedom overtook me for a few seconds until I hit the cold water and exhilaration took over.

I guess I found out the answer to Mom's eternal question, *"If your friends told you to jump off a bridge, would you do it?"* It's something my son would have done. I have a video of him jumping off a friend's roof on his skateboard. Foolishness isn't always a bad thing. Sometimes foolishness is just fun. I was learning fun, and I was having fun learning.

After we climbed out of the river, Onesimus, a full-time trail angel, met us in the middle of the bridge. With straggly blond hair, uneven beard, and flip flops, he looked more like a surfer than a former Army Delta Force soldier who retired to the trail. He followed the hiker bubble up and down the trail to help when he could. Onesimus decorated his RV with the Confederate flag and crucifixes, and today, the radio blared Glenn Beck's talk show. Onesimus is the name of the slave in the New Testament who ran away from his master and became a Christian. When I asked him if he was a Christian, he replied that he talked to God, but he didn't always listen. Onesimus is still running.

I spent little time in town as I resupplied, powered my cell phone, and returned to the trail. After I climbed up to the next vista, I noticed a solemn plaque dedicated to a four-year-old boy. In 1891, he wandered away from his school, walked seven miles to the top of the mountain, and died of exposure. *Grief and loss have been around for a long time.* I turned and walked away.

One last climb for the day. I stood at an intersection, unsure if I wanted to walk a half-mile off the trail to a shelter. When the weather turned to rain, I headed for the shelter. I was soaked by the down pour. Three guys joined me at the shelter after walking through the deluge. Two had thru-hiked the trail before and joined their friend for a section. One of them asked about shelter etiquette in the rain.

"Huh?"

"I mean we're all men, right?"

"Yeah."

"Then I hope no one has a problem with me taking a leak off the edge of the shelter."

"Okay, but I have to draw the line at number 2."

We just laughed. The rain on the metal roof was deafening. But much better to be under a metal roof than a nylon tent.

The climbs got easier. While other hikers talked about the difficult trail, no one wanted to go back to Georgia where everything seemed harder. My feet hurt, my back and knees ached, but I felt stronger. I passed another hundred miles and headed for nine hundred. After several days, I still hadn't had a legitimate shower, and I really didn't care. I hiked. I was becoming a thru-hiker. I still didn't call myself a thru-hiker, not wanting to jinx my hike. Trail Days was my conversion, Daleville, my baptism by fire, and my James River plunge was my baptism by immersion. I was a backpacker. I hiked, and I liked it.

Mr. Clean and Cruise Control caught up with me. They were two friends who'd met on the trail years before. Now, they arranged to do a section together each year. I collected dead branches after they invited me for a camp fire.

"Hey, guys, let me tell you about my son—he'd be about your age."

I tried to share my story about Aaron which. I wanted them to know that if I could trust God after losing my son then they might consider the same. They listened politely. Maybe they had to, maybe they wanted to.

I also met up with Forever, the other half of Waiting, who now hiked with a section hiker. Seeing the ex-partner so soon after seeing Waiting and her boyfriend seemed awkward. We headed into Waynesboro, a very hiker friendly town. Waynesboro has a proud history of manufacturing. Grand houses lined the streets and grander churches anchored its corners.

Southerner, a trail angel with gentile manners, picked us up on the edge of a busy road. I got ten percent off at a local restaurant, a free shower at the YMCA, and a place to stay at the Lutheran Church. I soaked in my first warm shower in over a week. The hostel offered sodas, chocolate-filled

Twinkies, and breakfast for a donation. *Chocolate-filled Twinkies, I love this country.*

The caretakers, a brother and sister team in their sixties, had thru-hiked the year before. Despite their age and shape, they talked about their hike with fondness. Now they gave back to the trail by taking care of the hostel. I ran into Miami Vice, the converted Buddhist I met with Blurbon back in Gatlinburg. I texted Blurbon, who was sidelined with an injury and would not return to the trail. After a resupply and a plate of lasagna, I hit the trail the next day.

Hikers talked about the Shenandoah National Park, my next milestone. They talked about the views, the groomed trails, and the waysides where you get something to eat. They didn't talk about the weather. The Smokies were feared by hikers, but the Shenandoah's were eagerly anticipated. Lori and I had spent part of our honeymoon along Skyline Drive, which meanders through the middle of the park. I blogged:

> The weather has to be better than the Smokies, and the trail
> couldn't be as difficult, but I know I will have a great experience.

I got one out of three right, but I would pay a small price.

CHAPTER 10

The Best Day of My Life

President Franklin Delano Roosevelt established the Shenandoah National Park where Lori and I honeymooned thirty-five years ago. This time the famed waterfalls and honeymoon lodges were different than I recalled.

After filling out the nonsensical hiking permit and stuffing it in the overflowing box, I moved down the trail. Throughout my entire hike, I saw rangers only four times: Twice in Shenandoah, and both times they were in a parking lot. Wherever I traveled, ranger stations and offices were closed due to budgetary constraints. Our national treasures are operating on shoestring budgets, but it did not deter my enthusiasm.

The wet trail soaked my shoes and the shrubbery soaked my shorts in minutes. Someone came up behind me and called my old trail name, "Wizard."

"Weatherman!" I exclaimed.

Weatherman was part of my original hiking group with Funk and Just Greg. This forty-something pharmaceutical researcher from Richmond looked twenty-something. Tall and lanky, he hiked fast and always knew the weather forecast. Weatherman had a case of recurring shin splints that caused him to take time off the trail. Old trail friends make the best hiking partners, so we hiked into the wet and put in twenty-two miles during our first day in the park.

Stopping at a well-kept three-sided shelter, a young happy hiker caught up to us. Coyote was short in stature, but he put in massive miles. He started his hike in late April and averaged twenty-seven miles from the outset. Coyote explained that he originally wanted to circumnavigate the world on a bicycle. He biked from Alaska to Argentina, over fourteen-thousand miles.

"I spent my first night in a frozen outhouse for truckers—no, you don't understand, I was really warm in there," Coyote said.

When Russia denied his visa, this physics teacher turned adventurer turned to the trail.

The next day, Weatherman and I hiked to one of the park's waysides for breakfast. Waysides are a series of three restaurants along the parkway that cater to park tourists. Each morning in the park, we hiked to pancakes, egg sandwiches, or biscuits and gravy. I didn't have time to make my routine oatmeal, but I was hungry and wanted to lighten my load. While we walked, I ate two packets of uncooked instant oatmeal. After chugging a packet, I mixed the recipe with a gulp of water. I chewed the oats long enough to take on the consistency and taste of peach wallpaper paste.

Three miles later, we got to the wayside. The smell of bacon, eggs and home fries filled the air. Spying a huge stack of pancakes on a customer's plate, I hovered over the innocent couple's breakfast order.

"Pancakes?"

The couple stared back at me. "Yeah, you can get your own up there," he said pointing at the counter.

After ordering, I headed to the bathroom where I found oatmeal flakes caked in my beard. *Oh my gosh, I look like a crazed old man.* After I cleaned up as best I could, I found a reason to go back and talk to the couple.

"Thanks for the tip about the pancakes." *Look, no oatmeal flakes,* I wanted to say, but the damage was already done. I found Weatherman, ate my own pancakes, and recalled the saying about first impressions.

After we left the wayside, a persistent mist overshadowed the park. My feet started to tingle as my new shoes rubbed the tops of my toes. The bottoms of my feet were as tough as alligator skin, but the tops of my toes were ill-prepared for the combination of cheap shoes and the raw, wet weather.

The month was May, and we were in the South. But we were in the mountains, and the rain made the weather seem even colder. An older female section hiker from St Louis had an even tougher outing on her second day in the woods. She seemed pretty gutsy taking on the elements alone on her first hike ever. She was exhausted but undaunted by her heavy pack. A small bear crossed our path and ran away while we talked. The brief encounter was my first bear sighting.

"What should I do if one gets close?" she asked.

"Run, or stand still, or look small, or stand on your toes, or raise your hands and yell," I said. "I heard all the above, and the only thing I know is the bears are more scared than us."

After another twenty-plus mile day, Weatherman and I dropped our wet packs in another shelter, which filled up with section hikers. Three recent graduates from Penn State played cards by the light of a battery-operated lantern. One hiker had graduated from the same small high school as my niece. The hikers' narratives sounded similar to other new hikers:

"How you doin'?" we'd ask.

"Not too good," would be the reply, "We didn't get too far."

"Oh, how far?"

"Eight miles from the last shelter," they'd reply.

"Eight miles, that's good for your first time out."

Weatherman and I waited until they asked us how far we hiked. With false modesty, we said, "Over twenty. But we've been doing this since March."

"And we're old," I added.

We smiled as they spilled out their overladen baggage onto the dusty shelter floor—a battery-operated camp light, playing cards, pillows, and heavy sweatshirts. One hiker asked how he could dry out his shoes.

"Wear them," Weatherman said. I laughed so hard I forgot about my sore feet. The hiker looked away and fell asleep.

The female hiker I met on the trail earlier came into camp and lightened her load by dropping her Clif bars on the wooden picnic table. We jumped on them like vultures.

After nine-hundred miles, I felt like a frontiersman who had grown an extra layer of skin—except on my feet. I wasn't just rising above my environment—I was becoming a part of my environment.

"Hiking is tough," I told the boys. "Life is tough. Like life, tomorrow you get up and face it. You hike out and find a way to like it. That's hiking, that's life." They weren't convinced.

The next day, Weatherman and I sat down at the next wayside where I tried biscuits and gravy to provide some added calories. I wanted a famed blackberry milkshake, but it was too early, and I was too cold and too wet. I gingerly walked away from the second wayside and into the rain with duct tape wrapped around my toes. When I walked, the pain subsided into a tingle and lingered in the background until I stopped to sit down.

Along the trail, an impromptu trail angel dressed in a clear rain poncho stopped Weatherman to tell him about a camp store that served hot coffee. After I bought an overpriced vial of Neosporin, we hung out to talk to Phil Phelan, a professional hiker, who made a living writing trail books and guiding hikes. He was in the middle of setting a record on another trail. Phil told us we might meet a friend of his, Scott Jurek, while he attempted to set an A.T. speed record. Phil also taped his feet with second skin and duct tape.

"You guys are rock stars," he told us to bolster our confidence, but I felt like an amateur. I was reminded of our conversation with the three young Penn Staters, except he was the pro now and we were the students.

After a second cup of coffee, I asked about the overpriced cabins. The manager told us a sixty-dollar cabin was available. The tight cabin had enough room for two sets of bunk beds and our wet gear. Using two Duraflame logs, we sat contented by the fire.

Less than ten miles that day, but our dusty little cabin was a palace—a respite from the trail I had touted like a tough frontiersman the day before. I love the trail, but I love being warm, and I love being dry even more. Weatherman brought in wet twigs, pine cones, and bark to keep a fire smoldering in the tiny woodstove while I focused on my feet. Sleeping with the aroma of burning wood in that hovel brought a peaceful end to a dreary day.

My feet were shades of red—freshly cracked and raw. They weren't bleeding, but the sharp pain increased when I took off the pressure from the duct tape and boots. Cheap hiking shoes didn't help, but the main culprit was the weather. My feet could have deteriorated into infection. Later, I met hikers who left the trail for weeks due to trenchfoot. Feet are everything, and after nine hundred miles, I paid the price for the wet mileage in my half-price hiking shoes.

The most important piece of gear a hiker owns is a good pair of hiking shoes. If your shoes are not right, your hike is all wrong. I had newfound respect for my wife, whose blisters were four times the size and depth of mine. She walked three times the distance but complained half as much.

Regrettably, the next day we left our quiet cabin and headed to complete the trifecta, our final wayside. While eating an egg sandwich, I got a glimpse of another small bear at a distance. Surprised to see one so close to the buildings in the light of day, I forgot to order that blackberry milkshake.

Just like the Smokies, good weather marked our first and final days in Shenandoah National Park. Weatherman and I were on our way to Terrapin Station Hostel. My old friend Tony and his son Rick, a recent cancer survivor, wanted to experience the trail. Rick, diagnosed with lymphoma the day he graduated from music school, had spent the last year battling the effects of the cancer and the poisons poured into his body. With his newfound love of life, he turned his attention to the trail. Tony and I have been friends for years. We cried together when I lost my son the same time Tony faced losing Rick. They could not put in long miles, so we planned a shorter schedule to let them get their trail legs.

Terrapin Station Hostel was a basement lined with homemade bunks made from two by fours, plywood, and vinyl mattresses. The place stretched the definition of hostel. The hiker special included two small frozen pizzas and a half gallon of ice cream. Partially eaten half gallons filled the freezer. I ate while the other hikers shared their expertise with Rick, who soaked up every word.

"Your friends did their homework, they showed up with the right equipment," one hiker said.

The next day Rick felt up for the challenge and hiked up the approach trail with me while Tony labored behind. Their excitement narrated the beauty of the woods.

"Dad, look at that view" … "Rick look at this" … "Oh, man, look at those rocks" … "I know, right?" Tony used his phone to video their hike. They were kids on an eight-mile field trip.

Tony struggled before getting into the rhythm of hiking. Father and son pointed out the rocks and the trees like they had never seen rocks or trees before. They took pictures and videos of each other hiking, eating, and taking breaks.

As the trail became more arduous, the effects of a year of chemotherapy pulsating through Rick's body became evident. The two stopped talking. Rick threw up his lunch, then his breakfast, then whatever was left, turning our field trip into a medical emergency. As the sun went down, we still needed to hike two more miles to a campsite that offered space and water.

Tony stayed with Rick, who could no longer carry his thirty-five-pound pack. I hurried ahead and dropped my pack, then ran back to the two and grabbed Rick's pack. I hiked his pack past my pack and ran back for mine. Meanwhile, Rick and Tony walked to my pack. We moved up the trail as I played leapfrog with the packs.

We staggered into our site in the dark. By ourselves, surrounded by foliage, and with water close by, we set up our tents and made dinner. Rick threw up the last of what was in his stomach while Tony and I sat on a log in front of a cold fire ring.

"I'm not saying you have to, it's your and Rick's decision, I said."

"It was pretty rough out there today," Tony replied.

"Tony, it's not going to get any easier."

"Let's see what tomorrow brings."

The next day, Rick's hip bothered him as he labored down the mountain. Still wiped out from the day before, we barely walked three miles before noon. After getting to a road, Tony called for a shuttle to go back to Terrapin Station.

Rick seemed like Aaron was behind me talking about the trees, the rocks, and the views. While I listened to this father and son on the trail together, I imagined Aaron and me. I found my voice quivering and my eyes tearing as I talked to Rick.

"Rick, I want to adopt you as my trail son. You reminded me of Aaron and how we would have had the same discussions as you and your dad."

"Hiking the trail is tough," he said, "But I still want to hike the A.T."

The three of us hugged and I made my way up the hill alone, turned and watched them drive away.

I was near the middle of this five-month, two-thousand-plus-mile odyssey. My legs felt heavy, my pace had slowed, and my vision was narrowed. Along the trail, I hunched over a warmed foil pack of stew while sitting on a soggy log in the rain. I missed my friends. Despite the time and the weather turning to rain, I walked seventeen miles before reaching a dank three-sided shelter at dark. Too tired to set up my tent, I crawled into my sleeping bag as a new hiker chattered about the trail.

"Should I set my alarm?" he asked.

"I guess I will," answering his own question.

"What time should I set my alarm for?" I heard him ask.

"Okay, I'll set it for nine," continuing his monologue.

Nine o'clock, nine o'clock? Who has to set their alarm for nine o'clock?

"Are you guys section-hikers?"

"Yeah, how could you tell?" asked the talker. "Was it the size of our packs or something I said?"

I was on the verge of rude.

"No, I just haven't seen you on the trail."

I turned over and shut my eyes. Like most nights, I could see Aaron. Some nights, I saw a boy trying to fill out an oversized little league uniform. Other times, I saw a twenty-nine-year-old man riding with me on a ski lift. Tonight, before I fell asleep, I saw him lying in a mortuary. The next day, I nodded to the talker who was quietly walking around the campsite when I headed out at 6:30.

I was on my way to the Roller Coaster, an infamous section in Virginia comprising several miles of drops and climbs. A weak smile came across my face as I thought of Aaron, who never shied away from a challenge— whether he snow boarded through the pines or skateboarded down the road. But the multiple twenty-mile days, leapfrogging packs, and the grind of backpacking for over two months had taken their toll. As I approached a thousand miles—a huge milestone—I just wanted the hike over.

I slipped on a moss-covered rock while crossing a stream and landed facedown in the water. My hands were wrapped in my pole straps and trapped underneath my chest. I saw one of my water bottles drifting down the stream and thought I was stuck. I pictured a hiker finding me days later, wondering how I could have been so stupid. I would become trail lore. So I got up and dragged my sorry self up the hill where I slumped beside the stones marking one thousand miles.

"One thousand miles, I walked one thousand miles," I repeated out loud, hoping to raise my excitement and feeling of accomplishment.

As I ate a peanut butter and spam sandwich, Twilight Zone and his hiking partner came by. They asked me to join them for a soda at Bear's Den Hostel, a famous mansion along the trail. As much as I wanted to, I trudged on alone. I met up with Dance Party, who was making his second thru-hike attempt after dropping out the year before. I told him, "I'm spent, I need to get off the trail." Later I wrote in my journal:

> As I approached the 1,000-mile mark, I sat down, called my new trail son (Rick), and ate a spam and peanut butter sandwich. Do I have anything left for the next 1,000?

I needed to stop at the headquarters for the Potomac Area Trail Council. The caretakers served lentil soup and sodas, then charged my cell phone. Twilight Zone joined me and said he heard from Dance Party that I was quitting.

"Not quitting," I resolved, "Just tired."

"That's good," he stated. "No one quits on me."

I was relieved to walk out of Virginia, the longest state along the Appalachian Trail, and into West Virginia, one of the shortest. Hikers looked forward to Harper's Ferry, the next town. They congregated in this fascinating town—chock-full of history, railroads, and waterways. Harper's Ferry buzzed with tourists, hikers, bicyclists, and paddlers. Harper's Ferry is also the headquarters for the Appalachian Trail Conservancy, where I searched the picture albums of hikers who already passed through town. Behind the cash register in an outfitter's store sat a lone bag of Epsom salts. I had to have them to soak my beleaguered body.

When I headed out of town, the trail utilized part of the Chesapeake and Ohio Canal. Its wide flat path had scores of weekend walkers who took curious glances at the thru-hikers with scruffy beards and unkempt hair. I was more interested in finding a motel room with a real tub.

With the extra pound of Epson salts in my backpack, I walked several miles to the next town. I almost cried when the motel manager told me the hiker special didn't include a bathtub. When he saw the pain in my eyes, he switched my room at no extra cost.

Soaking in a tub, followed by eating a club sandwich, buoyed my spirit. The next day, I walked through Maryland with newfound vigor. After the shortest state on the trail, I headed towards old friends and family. I wrote:

> I am also enjoying talking to close friends who continue to support me and encourage me. I am so blessed. One of the nicest things Lori ever said is that I have good friends. It's true. They

lift my spirits, make me laugh, and are good people. A Marine once described them as a good piece of gear, and now I get it. And they get me. I see the pain in their eyes when I talk about our loss. I see the joy in their eyes when I talk about our gain. I hurt; I hurt every day. The physical pain is a welcome distraction as each day I continue to cry out 'Why?'

I called a Marine friend, who I worked with years before. Fred was eager to see me and picked me up. Together we surprised John, another friend. After a great meal and another real bed, I walked out of Maryland. My optimism transcended the trail. Even though I really didn't know where I was, in Pennsylvania I was home.

My positive spirit got washed out by a brief storm. Wet feet suck, just no way around it. The rain stopped as quickly as it started. I found a campsite by an active stream.

I blogged:

> After being in civilization the past two nights, I'm lonely. Okay, I am very lonely. The good news is that I am in PA, and I am home. In two days, I should be halfway on the trail, and in four days, I should be in my old hometown. I hear they got their first traffic light. Darn civilization!

My confidence grew when I stood next to the sign marking the halfway point. A group of Boy Scouts gathered around me for a picture at this monumental point on the trail. Men hiking with boys gave me hope. Wilson, named for the volleyball, caught up to me.

"Why the volley ball?"

"Dunno," he replied. Wilson was an accountant from the Midwest who seemed to take on the trail in a logical, relaxed manner. We traded trail info. Eating a half-gallon of ice cream is a tradition at the halfway point at Pine Grove Furnace General Store. I have a strong objection to food challenges. Men in particular like to gross themselves out with food challenges in volume or temperature. I wanted no part of the challenge until Wilson, the level-headed accountant, told me he couldn't wait for it.

"Why?" I asked.

"Dunno."

"Me too," I said. Just like the James River challenge when I jumped off the railroad bridge, I jumped at the half-gallon challenge.

A spectator sat at the general store where the ice cream was sold. He wasn't a hiker—he wasn't even a worker at the park—he was a guy who liked talking to thru-hikers. I listened to his theory of the half-gallon challenge.

"Stay away from Chocolate Moose Tracks," he said. "And stay away from Cookies and Cream—way too heavy—they will weigh you down. You want something light. And don't get Mint Chocolate Chip."

"Why not?"

"I don't know what it is about the mint, but I've seen more chocolate chips hurled over that rail than any other flavor..."

I laughed. "So what do you recommend?"

"Neapolitan," he stated, "Think about it. You eat some vanilla, you move to the chocolate, you get tired of that, you try the strawberry, and you don't get sick of any one flavor."

Made perfect sense to me, so I bought Neapolitan. These days you can't buy a full half-gallon of ice cream. To add more misery after eating the modern container, tradition dictates you must eat an additional pint. And the park store balances its budget for another year. The Neapolitan went down easy. I chose blueberry for my last pint. Wrong choice. The final pint took longer to eat than the chocolate, vanilla, and strawberry combined.

After I finished my last bite, Wilson and I took our accolades, flat little wooden ice cream spoons printed with the words "half-gallon challenge," and waddled down to the lake. The month was June and many families were swimming or picnicking. Back at the general store, Turbo took on the challenge in record time while another hiker gave up after eating a third of his first carton. I respected his restraint, but I wondered if there was any correlation between quitting the challenge and quitting the trail.

That night, we stayed at the Pine Grove Hostel, a converted stone mansion, and the next day, Wilson and I headed our separate ways. My way headed home to Duncannon. Lori and I lived there for seven years before we packed up our three children, ages four to one, and headed back to graduate school in Indiana. Years later, we bought the family farm and moved back to Pennsylvania to give our children a sense of roots. Duncannon is a famous trail town and I was like a celebrity because I knew all the best places in this rural small town.

Again, I wrote:

...not to worry, because tomorrow I will be at my aunt's farm in Perry County. Now I am really getting close to home. I am so comfortable in the woods. I'm confident, not in myself really. Rather, I'm confident in life. Life just is. Life isn't fair—it just is. This I've always known, but now I am part of life. No longer needing to fight against it, but wanting to flow, to move with it. I am being looked after, even if it's a random piece of firewood, forgotten in the past, now bringing a modicum of comfort.

At Aunt Toot's house, I sat down with family to Pennsylvania Dutch chicken corn soup and strawberry pie. My cousin Steve followed my blog faithfully and whispered in my ear I was his hero. I teared up as I left their farm and climbed to Hawk Rock, which overlooked my little town of Duncannon sandwiched between the mountains and the Susquehanna River.

My feelings at that moment continue to resonate inside of me:

I have had some really good days, but I realize today is the best day of my life. When I climbed to the top of Cove Mountain and sat on Hawk Rock, I removed my hat because I was home. I climbed this trail over thirty years before with friends on a  Sunday and looked over this same view. Now I reached the mountain after walking from Georgia. The best day of my life is today. It always was and will be.

I walked with ease. Even the downhill felt good. As I walked into town, a vested gent greeted me with not a care in the world. I knew what I would do; I'd eat a hoagie then eat ice cream at the Dairy Bar where Lori used to work. I remember driving up after soccer practice in the summer from Messiah College to surprise her. I remember walking into the jewelry shop on the square to buy our wedding bands. I remember meeting friends at the pub. I remember running The Last Mile, a race around this old town, and I remember home.

I remember Aaron calling us after moving out and asking if he could come home. I cried that day. I handed him a paint brush and how hard he worked to get his life back. I remember Ali bringing home Jayden from the hospital for the first time. I remember my younger son Rob working for hours in the garage on his truck. I remember my sons laughing together and thinking life doesn't get any better than this. As I walked through town, I remember being John Leiter's son-in-law. I remember belonging. Being with family and friends tonight brought me home, brought me to the best day of my life.

I always smiled when my little grandson used to say that today is the best day of his life but now, I knew what he meant. Today is the best day of my life. Aaron is still with us, just as much as his younger sister and brother. The memories are still alive, so is hope, and so is he.

And now so am I—alive.

Jen and Trev picked me up, and I spent the night in Duncannon complete with family, friends, and my sister-in-law Tami's ham and green beans. When Lori answered my phone call, she was happy to hear where I was and thrilled to hear how I was doing. She had occupied herself with her routine of devotions, working out, and taking care of our house.

In the morning, I met my old friend Brian at Goodies Restaurant, complete with scrapple—a Pennsylvania Dutch staple. It's basically what is left over after they make hotdogs. Scrapple is a rectangle fried on a grill to the consistency of a MacDonald's hash brown. But just the right amount of syrup will make any hiker sing. I delayed saying goodbye to Brian, a Pennsylvania staple in his own right, for as long as I could. But the trail was calling me to the next best day of my life.

CHAPTER 11

When Will Sunday Smile

Buoyed by family and a hearty dose of Pennsylvania Dutch cooking, my legs were rejuvenated, and my spirit revitalized as I found a band of trail friends camped beside a small stream. I explained chicken corn soup and how to eat ham and green beans with a piece of buttered bread to my hiker family, and they explained sleeping at the Doyle Hotel. They told me about using their sleeping bag as a barrier between them and their mattress. One person even pitched their tent on their bed. Being with my trail family made me miss my real family more. I still had a long way to go through my home state and more friends remained ahead.

The next day I hiked to the 501 Shelter. The shelter is a cabin managed by a caretaker and renowned for its ability to have pizza delivery. Inside, old pizza boxes stacked four feet high and empty two-liter soda bottles filled three recycle bins.

Hikers complained about the rocks in Pennsylvania. The lack of trail maintenance made the rocky trails even more difficult. After talking to the caretaker about the condition of the shelter, I emailed the Appalachian Trail Conservancy about my concerns. Then I ordered a pizza and a steak sandwich.

The next day I headed for Port Clinton with cold pizza for lunch in my backpack. Twenty-five miles away lay Hamburg, which held its own memory for me. As I neared the next town, Port Clinton, a couple of groups of ultra-marathoners hustled up the trail dressed in clean, bright running shorts and singlets.

"Have you seen him, Scott Jurek?"

"Who?

"Scott Jurek. He's setting the A.T. speed record."

Mountain Squid said the last person to Katahdin wins.

While the A.T.C does not recognize speed records, Jurek wanted to break Jennifer Davis Farr's previous record of forty-six days. The trail is for hiking, not for racing; however, many groups enjoy the trail from hunters to hikers. By setting the record, he brought additional publicity to the trail, but the ultra-marathoners only saw the narrow path and missed the woods as they hurried past me.

Jurek passed me at Port Clinton, carrying nothing but purpose, surrounded by his team and a group that trailed behind him. He was rushed into a van to spend the night in Hamburg. He would eventually beat Farr's record by three hours. We were on the same trail, but other than waving to him as he sped by, we were in different worlds. The next day I went to Hamburg for a different reason:

> Today is Sunday, Father's Day. I will talk to my kids today. All my kids. All day. I am going back to Cabela's Outfitter store, the same one I visited at Christmas time to look for some hiking shoes. My wife told me I had to hike the trail after seeing the price of my new boots. She was looking through the racks while I stood at the edge of the balcony on the second floor when I heard Aaron call, "Hey Dad, Dad!" in his ten-year-old voice. I looked—but he wasn't there. A minute later his and his girlfriend's song played on the store intercom. I rushed down the stairs to find Lori. She shrieked after telling her, and I left the store with tears rolling down my face. Today I am going back.

Those who mourn sometimes encounter unusual experiences. I don't believe in ghosts—but I know what I heard. As a psychologist, I tried to understand what I heard, but as a father I didn't need an explanation. I took the voice as a comfort and as a way of staying connected to my son. Today I found myself back at Cabela's on Father's Day—not a coincidence, just another God-incidence, working his love and restoring mine. I walked around the store remembering last December.

On this day, I thought of my children who would think about me and their missing brother. I walked the aisles where no one knew my name, where I came from, or how I got there. Everything seemed artificial. The stuffed animals looked sad and the live fish looked trapped. I left without buying anything. Outside in the parking lot, cars spun me around, making me dizzy and wanting to be back in the woods.

My stop at Cabela's gave me a late start, but I wasn't concerned. I was supposed to be there on this day, now closer to my son and my family. After begging for a ride back to the trailhead, I called Lori. The conversation was brief—we both knew why. I put on my pack and hiked.

Two days and an exhilarating climb up the side of Lehigh Tunnel lay between me and the eastern edge of the state. The steep grade strewn with boulder-size rocks called for the skills of a rock climber. My heart pounded from exertion and sweat soaked my shirt. The sun shone bright. After countless climbs, this was the first time I worried about getting hurt. If I made the wrong decision, I would fall. And if I fell, I wouldn't stop falling for several hundred feet.

I can't believe the A.T.C. makes us do this. Sweat slipped down the small of my back and stones slipped down the side. Some hikers complained about the risks, but I welcomed the challenge. To push myself to the limits was why I was there. The climb over Lehigh Mountain pushed me to my limit. I looked above to a large cross painted on the top rock. The cross glorifying Christ lay juxtaposed to graffiti glorifying Joey & Jill, and the boyz.

As I climbed, I imagined tossing my hat over the side and watching its worn fabric float to the bottom. I wrote in my journal:

> I have an old hat I have worn from the start. My hat still looks good; she keeps the sun out of my face in sunshine and most of the rain. I got my hat early and thought her perfect. But along the way my hat no longer seems to fit. My hat is too hot when the sun is out and too heavy in the rain. My hair is longer, and my hat now fits tight around the brim, so I push my hat up on my forehead to make her work but she falls short. I have changed, I realize, but my hat has stayed the same. Yet, she tries so hard to fit, but I am not the same. I dressed her up with some turkey feathers to make her look good, but it doesn't change the basic problem. After I got to the top of the mountain today, I looked over the edge. I took off my old hat and imagined tossing her into the air like a Frisbee. I saw my hat getting caught in an updraft and floating away. I envisioned her settling on a tree

limb waiting for a hiker with the perfect head to start a new hike. But she was my hat. So I picked her up, figured a way to make her fit, and slogged on.

I am all the better for it.

Still morning when I reached the top, I sat down underneath a large pine and opened my Bible for a brief interlude. Sitting on top of a mountain on a sunny summer morning brought my world into focus. A subtle peace settled upon me before I hiked through more rocks and finding my way down the other side of Lehigh Mountain to Wind Gap.

Doug and Cathy from our home church arranged for a free meal for me at Ditzi's Tavern. Three brothers who played football at East Stroudsburg State University in the '70s owned the restaurant. I wanted to hear about their glory days, but they were more interested in the trail. Afterwards, I set up my tent behind the restaurant, and in the morning, they took me to the trailhead.

The next day, I hiked into Delaware Water Gap. In this quaint Pocono town, I reunited with my old high school soccer coach and his family. He moved to the Poconos after retiring from teaching. I had not seen Coach Hensel for almost forty years.

"Andy," he said

"Helmut?" I asked.

"Yeah."

"Helmut Hensel?" as if there could be another Helmut in Delaware Water Gap.

Coach Hensel taught me how to play soccer, took me on college trips, showed me how to shoot a gun, and took time to mentor me during my adolescent years. One of his sons gave me a T-shirt to wear for dinner that said "Iron sharpens iron."[5] After walking through seven states, we toured his farmette where I'd stayed almost forty years before. Being reunited with him and his wife, Geni, was another blessing of my pilgrimage.

My stop at Delaware Water Gap allowed my nephew Luke to drive up the next day. He drove me south to his house where my twin sister Beth picked me up to take me home to North Carolina. I wanted to be at our family reunion in Emerald Isle, North Carolina. The trail had a way of working things out. For a week, I laid in the sun at the beach, went boating on the sound, and shot skeet at the range.

I changed on the trail, but I didn't put what I learned into practice at home where it mattered most. I was changing, but my hat was still the same. I became petty and controlling when things didn't go my way. The lesson of letting God's plan reveal itself and letting things go faded into the woods when I faced the stark realities of beach life. I wasn't ready to be home.

Again, I blew my chance to be a supportive husband. I got along with everyone but Lori. We were both happy to see each other but didn't get a chance to really talk. I hustled each day to make sure everyone was having a good time, but I neglected the person who mattered most. My expectations were unrealistic, and I was on edge the entire time. By the time I left, we were not talking. The trail is tough, but real life is tougher. With a pack full of regrets, I headed back to the trail.

Lori and our grandson Jayden were going to bring me back to the trail and hike with me, but that changed over the course of the week. My brother Tom drove me back to Delaware Water Gap. As I walked across the Delaware River and into New Jersey, I started the familiar process of climbing up another mountain. Late in the day, I reached Sun Fish Pond. Now I found myself alone, staring at this quiet little pond. I felt selfish and guilty as I pictured Jayden fishing at the pond. Children have such faith when fishing. They stare at the water with certainty they will catch a fish. Today I kept walking.

The trail got rocky again as I passed the pond and found a site to pitch my tent, make dinner, and hang my bear bag. I called the family of one of Aaron's friends in Pennsylvania. Aaron wasn't the only Pennsylvania transplant living in Colorado. His friend Roger moved to Keystone for the work and the snow. Roger's family insisted on coming out to the trail and bringing me back to their house for dinner and a warm bed. The next day they put me back on the trail as the weather started to rain.

New Jersey isn't known for its bear population. Jersey is famous for its beaches. Most people are surprised New Jersey has bears. I spent many summers in Ocean City, New Jersey, and did not know that such a populated state had such wilderness. So I wasn't confident when I hung my bear bag the first night back on the trail. The last time I saw a bear was in the Shenandoahs, but the smallish animal looked harmless. I'd heard stories of bear encounters, and I didn't need one of my own. Mice in the shelters scared me more than bears.

In my journal, I wrote:

> I am amazed at the beauty of New Jersey. I lived in South Jersey for four years and knew that Jersey is more than beaches and highway, but I didn't know the Garden State is small mountains and forest. I met up with some friendly hikers and spent the night at a well-built stone shelter. Being with others made being away from family easier, but I am ready to finish this hike and get back to familiar surroundings.

But God was not finished.

The mountainous southern states were a distant memory. I had now walked through most of the Mid-Atlantic States. I reasoned that time would fly by in New England. What I found was a moment takes forever but goes by in a blink. I needed to stay in the moment, to rise above my circumstances, yet savor the experience. A moment is a gift.

I passed men hiking with their children. The sight filled me with so much emotion I made a point to stop and tell the dads they were doing a good thing. I doubt if they understood, but someday they will. Someday they will understand what I have grown to appreciate—the moment. I concerned myself with the next minute and forgot the moment-to-moment pleasure of my kids catching a fish or missing a fly ball.

Living in the moment and unconditional love mystified me. One time at a men's meeting, a guy said, "Think of your kids."

"I am," I exclaimed. "That's why I don't get it."

I laughed, but I was serious. Well, that changed on July 27, 2014. At that moment, when Lori pounded her tears into the floor and I stood over her, nothing else mattered. Our son was dead and nothing, nothing mattered. Grades, college, even table manners didn't matter. All of that is vanity. Life—life mattered, nothing else. Unconditional love became real on the twenty-seventh.

Life on the trail mattered, but life was too brief in Jersey. New Jersey knows how to build boardwalks at the shore and on the trail. At one well-maintained shelter, I struck up a conversation with Tiger Bob and Bee Stinger, two hikers who were a few years older than me.

Bee Stinger got his trail name because his last name sounded similar to his name. He was a tall sixty-something, who looked older due to a grey comb over and neck hair that grew longer than his silver beard. His Indiana accent and woodsy euphemisms could make anyone smile. His wiry frame bounded down mountains like a kid late for dinner. Tiger Bob's trail name, orange T-shirt, and tiger handkerchief told of his devotion to the Clemson Tigers. He deviled us with his quiet southern drawl. The three of us shared a desire to improve our love of God and others and walked at the same pace, so this trio of old men hiked together the next day.

I hadn't hiked with a partner since Weatherman left the trail in the Shenandoahs due to his shin splints. He did not return to the trail. A hiker leaving the trail was always a sad day. The disappointment and indecision showed on their faces. No one wanted to leave the trail due to injury. They put so much effort into preparing and hiking, and now they were leaving early. Tiger Bob had left the trail the year before with a perforated ulcer. He returned to the same spot to complete his hike and hiked alone until meeting up with me and Bee Stinger.

We had similar goals, but I felt like I had a sign across my forehead that said, "Fragile. Keep Upright." By now I realized finishing was not as important as the journey. Hiking made me savor the moment and take time for those around me.

The journey made the trail special. The trees often looked the same, hardwood or pine. Even many of the vistas looked similar. My routine of hiking, eating, and sleeping became repetitious. What made the trail unique was picking out trees with peculiar shapes that Tiger Bob said were similar, and huge rocks that Bee Stinger said were out of place. I saw the uniqueness, the similarities, and the relationships of creation working together.

Everything had its place, and I was part of it.

I wore the same synthetic black T-shirt, shorts, and a pair of wool socks with liners. At night, I washed my laundry in a stream, and in the morning, I put on wet clothes, changed my socks and hung the wet pair from my pack. I smelled something awful, but it didn't matter. Jennifer Davis Farr, the previous A.T. speed record holder, said she could always tell a thru-hiker by the smell when she approached them on the trail. Hygiene comprised of getting wet in a stream and brushing my teeth at my campsite. I found my place when life got simple. United with my world, I hiked with a united group.

After getting to a road, I stuck out my thumb and the first car stopped to give us a ride into Vernon, New Jersey. We stayed at the Lutheran Church where they gave us a room, food, laundry, and showers.

The climbs got steep after crossing into the well-maintained trails of New York. Pennsylvania had its rocks, New Jersey had its boardwalk, and New York had its delis. Delis near the trail meant a great sandwich and a pack of Drake's cupcakes. Drake takes the junk out of junk food and puts back nothing but good.

We bought the five-dollar special from an eighty-year-old man at a hot dog stand—two hot dogs and a Coke before walking down the road for ice cream. A woman standing behind us at the parlor was a former thru-hiker and paid for our ice cream cones. These random acts of kindness continued to encourage me to trust others.

Forever of Forever and Waiting showed up at the ice cream parlor. Disheartened to be hiking solo, she slack-packed and took alternate trails to increase her miles and her motivation. Her methods weren't working. Her eyes told me she thought about leaving the trail. I told her I thought about quiting every day, then I told her about my vision:

> I picture myself at Mt Katahdin, Maine. I envision seeing the sign, tears fill my eyes as I reach for the wooden cross necklaces Lori and I got back in Virginia. As I get closer, my knees get weak and I reach for my son's Keystone knit hat I have carried since Georgia. I fall to one knee balanced by my poles. I pray, I weep, I am done.

After telling her my vision, I asked Forever to hike with us, but I never saw her again.

My vision of finishing played in my head along the trail and in my tent. Quitting also went through my head. But I replayed my vision until finishing became my reality.

The next day I was leading our trio when from a distance, we spotted a flock of ruffled grouse making their way along the ground.

"Grouse!" I exclaimed.

Inexplicibly, another hiker heading south leapt from behind a tree.

"THEY'RE TURKEYS, MAN! TURKEYS!" he shouted at short distance. His words blasted me like a double-barreled shotgun, and I lost my face to a pattern of word pellets. I didn't want to fight over game birds, so I walked away, flabbergasted, looking at the ground, and muttering to myself. Tiger Bob said he never saw me look so shocked and speechless.

Bee Stinger brought up the rear and began a series of negotiations with the New Yorker, who was convinced he knew his wildlife. The two negotiated a détente of sorts and decided that the man saw turkeys earlier, and we later saw grouse. Tiger just laughed.

Does it really matter? I walked north.

We came out of the woods and into a weekend crowd vacationing at Bear Mountain Park. The trail proved arduous for out-of-shape weekenders who climbed the stone steps up Bear Mountain to its observation tower. Thru-hikers looked like unkempt time travelers scattered between the tourists. We lifted our knees up the stone steps as the multitude labored along their short hike. We had hiked from Georgia, but the day-hikers were having a difficult time walking from the parking lot.

In New York, the A.T. had delis, and New York had a zoo. The trail goes right through the middle of a zoo. We walked through a park crowded with cookouts and into Bear Mountain Zoo. Once we were in the woods avoiding bears, now they stared at us from behind bars.

Walking into the woods used to worry me. Now the placid woods brought relief as we walked across the congested Palisades Bridge. I longed for the woods where life moved at my pace.

We left the barbecues, music, and people behind as we climbed past trail maintenance crews. A crew member told us about a hiker feast at the next shelter. We arrived at the RPH shelter, which stands for Ralph's Peak Hikers, before dinner and set up our tents around the site. Several hikers joined us at the shelter, some of whom stayed a few days to help with the maintenance.

One hiker told me he just got out of a Philadelphia jail. He seemed convinced that Warlocks, members of a Philadelphia motorcycle gang, stayed on the trail looking for people. To be safe, I heeded his advice and avoided him for the rest of the evening.

I had craved a root beer float for several days and to my amazement, root beer floats were on the menu for dessert. *God is good.* I smiled through my second float. The caretaker of the shelter lived three miles away and invited us for breakfast the next day. Maybe life is good after all.

In the morning, Bee Stinger stayed behind to hike with another hiker named Fig while Tiger Bob and I hiked on waffles and coffee for seventeen miles. We ended up at a garden nursery, which allowed hikers to stay on their property. I washed my clothes by wearing them in the outside shower powered by a garden hose. Then we walked up the road to another deli that sold hoagies for dinner. Bee Stinger showed up after I set my tent in a line of tents squeezed between railroad tracks and an open access highway.

Just a few feet from the road and tucked behind some trees, our fringe society carried our homes on our backs and lived off the kindness of strangers. Headlights from the trucks and horn blasts from the trains kept me up most of the night. In the morning, Tiger and I packed up and moved to the next state.

The White Mountains, the jewels of the trail, remained ahead, but I still had several states before attempting its above-tree-line ascents. The Whites are famous for drastic weather changes and epic vistas. With the Whites on my mind, I walked into Connecticut not realizing the challenge that lay before me.

In the east, summer heat means high humidity. Now, even the mountains couldn't hide us from the heat. My clothes were not just wet, they were soaking wet, and hung on my frame like a weathered scarecrow. We were in a heat wave. Sweaty salt chafed both arms and legs. I'd rather sweat than shiver, but the heat became unbearable, and the bugs made matters worse. Small bugs, barely seen, made their living annoying my face. The carbon dioxide I exhaled attracted them, but I couldn't do much about that. Mosquitoes converged on me whenever I stopped, and trail flies hovered around my ears.

Bee Stinger swore at them, "Gosh dang it," and Tiger Bob just laughed, pretending to be unaffected. Hikers sometimes leave the trail at this point after going almost fifteen hundred miles. Incredible that they would give up after coming so far, but the miles, the terrain, and the weather wears out hikers.

Bee Stinger was slowing down, and his enthusiasm lessened. He detoured into Kent while Tiger and I bypassed the chance for a resupply. I had food enough for meals, but I had little for snacks throughout the day. The sweat poured from me, taking along precious calories. I drank as much as I could, but lactic acid filled my heavy legs. I bottomed-out—I bonked.

I thought I could hike hungry, but I was wrong. Hungry is not just a feeling in your stomach, but affects everything from muscles to motivation, and I was running out of both. Just like an old car sputtering as it coasts into the next gas station, I needed fuel.

Tiger Bob went ahead while I stopped to make myself a small pot of pasta and tuna for dinner. Alone on a fallen tree, I stirred my simmering noodles and orangeaid. Taking in some food and reflecting on the day was enough to revive my sagging spirits. After I got up and hiked along the last of the twenty-two miles for the day, I bounded into our next camping area.

"We can't let that happen again," Tiger insisted. "It's all in your head."

"You should be a wizard," I replied.

A third hiker joined the camp site and told us most of his life story. His pronounced stutter made understanding him difficult. He hiked the trail because he couldn't get a job after his third DUI. *Three DUI's?* Tiger and I looked at each other as the hiker blamed the state for his troubles. With three strikes on his record, he was considered a felon, and jumped on the trail to escape his life.

Since we bypassed Kent, we had ten more miles to the next resupply in Salisbury, a trendy New England town. Trendy in New England means expensive and overpriced. I got my bill in the checkout line and looked at the supermarket cashier as if she had completed my prostate exam, so I returned my eight-dollar jar of designer peanut butter.

Bee Stinger gave me an enthusiastic fist bump when he rejoined us in town. Due to hygiene, hikers don't hug—hikers bump fists. Bee stopped in Kent to get a medical checkup and discovered he had Lyme Disease. He often complained about his physical condition, but now he really was sick. He was lethargic but also determined to continue his hike and added antibiotics to his long list of dietary supplements.

Bee had lost over fifty pounds since starting the trail despite carrying a hefty amount of food. He talked calories throughout the day and fretted about his next resupply. His family mailed him pounds of powdered nutrients on a regular basis. One time when he wasn't looking, I tried to lift his pack, but I didn't get far.

Bee Stinger was the extrovert of the group, who always stopped to talk to hikers. He had a quirky sense of humor. Every morning, he looked at his backpack sitting on the ground and commanded, "Jump up, jump up." Every morning. He must have been the only guy on the trail who smelled worse than me. Maybe the cause was the supplements. Now his lack of energy caused him to withdraw. He still talked, but his enthusiasm waned. The disease extracted a toll on his body and spirit.

In my journal, I recalled:

> I have not had a real shower in a long time and laundry is an even more distant memory. Yet, I am growing in confidence, speed, and endurance. I have been reading about Paul's travels spreading the gospel, living on his own skills, and enduring great hardships knowing he would pay the ultimate sacrifice. What strength, courage, and conviction he had. I still find myself in weak moments but reach out to God moment to moment.

While Bee Stinger lagged behind to hike with Fig, Tiger Bob and I met my brother Tom, sister-in-law Clare, and her sister Tanya near Beckett, Massachusetts. As slow as I hiked before Salisbury, my speed doubled as I marched to meet my family. They understood that hiking miles is not an exact science, but I did not want to hold up my big brother. We passed a large sign on the trail that read, "Welcome Home, Bubble Butt," but I was pretty sure the sign was not meant for me. I had to double over the band on my shorts just to keep them up.

When Tom picked us up, he put a blanket across the back seat because of our muddy condition.

"Andy, you really stink," he said as we drove to his sister-in-law Tanya's house.

"I know, Tom, you told me. Three times."

"But you really—" he started.

"I know, I know," I interrupted.

It had been a week since I took an outdoor shower without soap and I wore my clothes. I only carried hand sanitizer on my shoulder strap and considered soap as extra weight.

When we arrived at the house, Tom's wife Clare, in good Greek fashion, cooked way too much food.

"Clare, root beer floats for dessert! You read my blog!"

"We follow your blog every day."

After a short night in a real house, Tom left me at a trailhead for the second time. Even though we were dry, clean, and well-fed, I asked him, "Are you really going to make me get out of the car?" A day before, I had to sit on a blanket because I stunk and now that I had a shower, he was making me get out. We were ready, we thought, for the rest of the trail or, at least, the rest of Massachusetts.

Tiger Bob looked forward to being reunited with his wife in Dalton, Massachusetts. The trail took a flatter trajectory at a lower elevation, which meant more wear, more roots, and more mud. Tiger bounded up the mountains without stopping until the last sharp climb. I was usually stronger on the up-hills, but now he was the one anticipating family.

It was Sunday again, the day the officer walked up my path and I was walking closer to the one-year anniversary of Aaron's death. Tears filled my eyes. *Am I moving on or moving backwards?*

My attitude was just as perplexing for those around me because my emotions changed in a matter of minutes. Sometimes I was quiet and distant for hours of miles, absorbed in my thoughts. Sometimes I snapped at slight pokes from my trailmate. I did most of my crying at night, but my tears spilt onto the trail. Tiger pretended not to notice.

Word along the trail told me there was a house in Dalton where I could camp for free while Tiger stayed at the motel with his wife. Being part of the thru-hiking community meant sharing news as we neared a town. After getting into Dalton, I found the man who had offered his yard to thru-hikers for the past thirty-six years. His tired, five-minute prepared speech focused on keeping quiet so as not to disturb his neighbors. I asked him if he was getting burned out. He replied he had problems in the past two years with hikers being loud, leaving trash, and disrespecting his home.

As I set up my tent, the owner pulled his car into the driveway and out jumped Waiting from the previous hiking duo, Forever and Waiting.

"Hey, Phantom!" she exclaimed.

"Hey, Waiting!" I called back to a chorus of "SHHHUUUUSH" from the owner. I had to laugh. After I got set up, I crawled in my tent before the clouds thundered and rained again. This time, I felt secure as I reflected on the Sabbath and what Sunday could mean. I called several friends and family to sound out my thoughts. Lori was doing well. I joked that she didn't need me, but in some ways, being apart was easier. Being apart allowed me time to think about all of the trivial things I let cloud my day.

"Do you want to be right or do you want to be married?" my supervisor in grad school would ask.

The next day, I packed up my wet gear and headed to the motel in town. Tiger was zeroing so I zeroed for the first time since getting back on the trail. Tiger Bob met his wife and friends from Mercy Flights, for whom he raised thousands of dollars by hiking. Adding to my joy, Bee Stinger showed up, so we shared a room. His talkativeness returned, Bee was on the mend, and I would have to listen.

I used the resupply in Dalton to eat, sleep, do laundry, and catch up on blogging at the town library. I met a section-hiker from Colorado, eight years my senior, who motivated me to pursue my dreams. When I first got on the trail, I saw so many possibilities for my life. As time marched on, I discarded many of my dreams. I got more realistic and narrowed my scope.

I wrote:

> I will keep the aperture as open as possible and maybe someday,
> Sunday will smile again.

Bee Stinger told me he wanted to slow down when we left in the morning. He sounded like he was breaking up with us. Tiger Bob said goodbye to his wife, and we were off to hike the trail. I have always been the emotional one, so departing on Monday, I choked up even though Tiger was saying goodbye and not me.

The trail, littered with leaves and bits of pine bough, gave the forest a scent of evergreen. Tulip, beech, and maple trees, along with the hemlock, painted the landscape. Blueberry-like plants that looked like small ceramic balloons on taut wire lined the trail. We hiked toward Mount Greylock, the highest peak in Massachusetts. The trail was not steep but had its share of rocks, roots, and mud. A typical climb, yet I found myself unable to keep up with the others and fell to the rear.

We put in some big miles, and I thought they were wearing on me, but I was in the midst of more—I was in grief. As I got closer to the one-year anniversary of my son's death, every Sunday, the day he died, was more emotional and exhausting.

The side effects of my grief seemed like the side effects of Rick's cancer, which he had to rid from his body.

Grief is like that—you lose someone good, and your body needs to rid itself of the lingering poison. You cry, you stare, you feel lethargic, you wait, then you try to get on with life. Yet, life has changed forever.

When we made our way to the impressive tower at the summit of Greylock, I was lightheaded, my reactions delayed, and my stomach queasy. My emotional release, matched with the exertion of the trail, proved painful. The only thing to do was to pick up my pack and walk.

I walked down to a shelter in a brief rain I no longer feared. The rain came harder the faster we ran to the shelter.

"Missed it by that much," I said in my best Maxwell Smart voice.

My legs were heavy, my ankles sore, and I carried a load that would never go away. Surrounded by other hikers in the shelter provided a momentary relief from my storms as I prepared for another round tomorrow.

CHAPTER 12

MOUNT KILLINGTON MIRACLE

> Today the pine forest took on a Christmas look and smell.
> If I shut my eyes, I can see my young kids on Christmases past
> dancing in delight over the simplest of gifts; always so grateful,
> ever so kind. The month is still July.

Tiger Bob and I hiked up and down Mount Williams, then up and down Mount Prospect. They are shorter than Greylock, but as we climbed they proved just as steep and difficult. All the ascensions of the Appalachian Trail equal summiting Mount Everest sixteen times. If you climb Mt Everest once, you get your name in the paper. If you climb the Appalachian Trail, you get to go home.

After crossing into Vermont, we surpassed the sixteen-hundred-mile mark. Instead of counting how many miles I hiked, I began counting how many miles were left—six hundred.

Vermont provided us with a first. Hiking southbound down the trail came two nudists wearing nothing but their backpacks and shoes. That's right, not a stitch, nothing, buffo, nunca, nada, birthday suits, and naked as a jaybird. I think they wore shoes.

An overweight man and woman in their early sixties casually walked by us and said hello.

"Uh, hi," I might have said, I can't recall. Then I looked back to watch Bee Stinger's doubletake.

"You checked him out, Bee Stinger."

"I did no such thing."

"Did too."

"Well, you did, too," he replied.

We laughed like school boys, figured they were a new type of ultralight hiking, and moved on at a quick pace—a very quick pace. We did twenty-one-miles that day and nested by another great brook. I fell asleep to the sounds of water churning over the rocks wondering if the Vermont ultralight movement was going to catch on at our North Carolina beach back home.

Vermont's topography is like the frosting on a cake, one short peak after another without ever getting to a defined summit. The top is a flattened affair lush with trees, denying us a view. We climbed a fire tower at noon to see the vast stretches of wilderness still left in the northeast.

After climbing on a fallen tree, Tiger Bob yelled, "Ride 'em cowboy!"

Not to be outdone, I jumped on the tree yelling, "Yee Haw!" and fell into the mud on the other side. Bob looked back at me, perplexed.

"Got thrown," I said sheepishly as I made my way to my feet.

More rain. The clouds rained hard enough to fill in the mud holes on the trail with water. As we scrambled along the sides in fruitless attempts to keep our feet dry, we succumbed to the muddy quagmire. Bee Stinger fell into one pit and climbed out looking like a barnyard animal.

"Gosh dang it," he yelled in his southern Indiana accent.

The rain didn't stop when we did, so we put our tents up in the wet. To keep the inside dry, I reversed the normal process by putting up the rain fly, a nylon tarp that covers the tent, then getting underneath the tarp to raise the tent body. After I was dry, and fed, I listened to the comforting rain patter on my tent while lying in my sleeping bag. Bee Stinger snored in his covered hammock and Tiger Bob and I talked through our tents, pitched only a foot apart, before falling asleep.

The happiest day on the trail is resupply day—always. With a pack lightened by the absence of food, I shifted into a higher gear, knowing that tonight I would get a real meal and sleep in a real bed. Before walking into hiker-friendly Manchester, we climbed another fire tower to get a view of the ski mountains and the lakes below. Without fire towers, I would never have known what Vermont looked like. I climbed the tower atop Mount Stratton where Benton McKay first got his vision of creating the Appalachian Trail almost one hundred years prior.

The Appalachian Trail is an American accomplishment. McKay never intended or even imagined thru-hiking the trail in one year. He foresaw a series of huts for people to retreat to from their urban existence and reconnect with nature. While the trail changes from year to year, the challenge remains the same. It's still the trail.

I thanked McKay as I hiked into Manchester. My wife would describe the town as, "Cute, cute, cute." A lively woman in her seventies pulled over and asked if we wanted a ride. We would have hurt her feelings if we turned her down. While driving to a restaurant she put a CD into her player. Her music was a compilation of bawdy songs set to popular tunes. She selected a song called "Mammaries I Desire" set to Billy Joel's "We Didn't Start the Fire." She sang along, complete with hand gestures. We just laughed when she wanted us to sing along but worried each time her gestures took her hands off the steering wheel.

Her husband lived in a nursing home and after visiting him each day, this trail angel drove around town chauffeuring hikers. When she let us out, she had to show us her beach towels of life-sized sunbathers. We walked away with smiles on our faces to get resupplied and dinner.

In the morning, Tiger Bob, Bee Stinger, and I worked together to make a fitting breakfast at a hostel just outside of town. Bob made pancakes, I made eggs, and Bee cleaned up. We made a good breakfast and a better team. We needed both when we climbed Mount Bromley that morning.

As we climbed through the woods, the trail led us up along the edge of a long narrow clearing. I took a few minutes to realize we were in the middle of a ski run with ski lifts overhead and my thoughts drifted to Aaron. I lagged behind the others as my mood moved to somber. When I got to the summit, the ski lifts and runs surrounded me. I sat on a concrete pad imagining Aaron riding a snowmobile to a job, climbing a tower, and getting the lift moving.

In the past, I had had several conversations with Tiger Bob about Aaron, and today I told Bee Stinger about him.

"This must be unpleasant for you," Bee stated.

"No, just the opposite," but for the rest of the day I walked alone. The pain hurt good. Sometimes grief is like that—painful, but that's how I wanted it. Sometimes hurting just felt good. The scene hurt my heart, but I wanted to be immersed in Aaron's world. Mount Bromley was just a foreshadowing of what awaited me at Mount Killington just a few days away.

After a couple of miles, we found a site near a stream, and Bee Stinger found two trees to hang his hammock. Bee Stinger, ever the optimist, exclaimed, "I like this better, this is what you can do when you are thru-hiking." The location was quiet, free, and ours.

In the morning, a gentle rain started our hike. The trail crossed a road where Qu's Whistle Stop Restaurant, an old train station, served lunch. Bee Stinger told us he couldn't keep up the mileage and wanted to hike with Fig and Grizzly One. I understood Bee's feelings. He said he had to rush and couldn't relax knowing we were always ahead of him. Bee Stinger had kept Tiger and me connected with the rest of the trail community by making it his mission to talk to everyone who crossed his path. We didn't want to lose him.

After we broke from lunch, Tiger marched ahead, and Bee Stinger and I bumped fists. I never saw him again. The next day, I would climb Mount Killington. Despite what I wrote in my journal, I wasn't prepared for what would happen:

> I am reconciling with the fact that tomorrow is the one-year anniversary of my son's death in a traffic accident. I forced myself not to cry or dwell on the ugliness today. I did not want to deal with it. I pushed myself in another direction, called my family, ordered flowers for Lori, and now I am in bed waiting for the start of just another day.

My legs quivered, my pace slowed to an all-time low. *What is happening?* Roots grabbed at my feet, rocks brushed at my shins. *This has to be the hardest climb.* Somewhere in the distance was Tiger Bob. *I'll never catch him ... Don't think—just walk.*

I tried to disengage and separate from my feelings, but my effort was futile. I went through the motions; my walk was mechanical. Grief is like sleepwalking. I sleepwalked, but even sleepwalking hurt. The roots looked large, the rocks ridiculous, and my pace pathetic. Tiger waited for me at another broken-down shelter.

We ate a snack at the shelter, I looked at the vista through reddened eyes. Two hikers told us about the side trail to the Mount Killington ski lodge. I didn't want to hold Bob back, but something pulled me toward the ski mountain.

"Wanna go?"

I nodded my head and started the rock scramble up the hill.

The narrow, steep climb took longer than I expected. I took a picture of the clouds when we got to the top. Later, I discovered the clouds were in the distinct shape of an angel, a sign of things to come.

We climbed down the other side and picked our way to the ski lodge, which opened for lunch. The lodge looked like Summit House at Keystone, Colorado, where we held the Celebration of Life service for Aaron. The noisy gondola made its rounds while we waited for lunch. I imagined two hundred people coming up the lift to be at Aaron's celebration. Tears poured out of me. *Why? Why, God, why?*

One year ago, I sat lifeless at his Celebration of Life service with my little poem in one hand. Lori's hand was in the other. In front of me were a few pictures, a pocketknife, and a black, fake-leather urn that looked more like a hotel ice bucket. Beside me were Lori, Ali with Jayden, and Robby, our youngest. Two hundred others behind me looked over the pictures, past the urn, out a wall of glass, and onto the slopes and ski lift that Aaron fixed for a living.

I made my way to the microphone. Some faces stood out while the rest blurred into a background of aspen and ski posters. I read my poem, *Mamma Let Your Boy Grow Up to be a Cowboy.* I sat down not noticing Ali, his sister, getting up.

"I don't like talking at these things," she told the group with a quivering voice and tear-stained cheeks. "Aaron always went to Jay's games. One day, he saw a little girl struggling with a big bag of soccer balls on the steps. He looked at her dad behind her and said to him, 'I guess chivalry is dead.' A minute later, we were at the car, and my big brother opened my door. 'Chivalry is only dead if you let it die, Big Al,' he whispered." She sat down.

Someone spoke, someone sang, someone prayed, someone said goodbye. We hugged, we laughed, but laughter is hollow when laughing isn't surrounded by smiles—and no one smiled. Not real smiles. We ran out of Kleenex, and we said goodbye to each other, but we didn't say goodbye to Aaron.

It was still morning on Killington when I ate a soggy hamburger wet with grease and grief. I was a wreck. We hiked down the mountain and past several houses. At a small inn, boaters and swimmers enjoyed the sunshine and lake. I sat by myself on a log eating a miserable peanut butter and spam sandwich. I wasn't hungry, I just didn't know what to do with myself. The time was too early to stop, so I put my pack on for the last time that day. After getting more water, we hiked up one more mountain.

When will this end? When will this end? Asking why leads nowhere, but today I was going nowhere and kept asking, *Why, why him, God, why? Why not me? Why couldn't I take his place?*

On my Appalachian pilgrimage, I met others who'd lost children: George in Damascus who lost a son and Rick in Duncannon who lost a daughter. They all said the same thing; "It hurts, and I don't have the answer." Sometimes they hugged me. And somehow that helped.

Today Tiger was less than five yards behind me, but I was by myself as we climbed our last mountain. At five-thirty, we dropped our packs at a powerline clearing, ten yards from and in full view of the trail. I thought my day was behind me. Mount Killington's ski runs loomed in the distance before as I bent down to get my tent poles. They were gone.

"What the—" I shouted in a loud un-Christian-like manner, "I'm screwed!"

After four months, I had a system. I packed each item in its place. Everything in my pack and in this world has a purpose and a place, everything counts. Losing my tent poles was a game changer. If I didn't get them back, my tent wouldn't work. After eighteen hundred miles, my pole bag fell out of an eight-inch-deep pocket. I needed them. I told Bob not to expect me until after dark.

Armed with only a cellphone, I ran into the woods. Twenty yards into the woods I saw something that took my breath away and jerked me into reality. Shoulder-high on a tiny nub on a sapling hung my tent poles. *How did they get here?* I saw no one on the trail. No one passed by Bob or me. If my tent poles fell out, how did Bob not see them lying on the trail? Grabbing on to them as if they weren't real took me from reality to spirituality. I held them close, then I lifted them to the sky.

"Oh God, oh Aaron, thank you, thank you!"

Today I felt the presence of God. I believe in angels, I don't believe in ghosts, but I do believe in the supernatural. I never felt so close to God since I walked down the middle of Folcroft Union Church when I was in junior high. Whenever I heard people talking about experiencing a miracle, I looked for alternative explanations. Now I confronted the inexplicable. I grabbed the poles and raised them to God.

"Thank you, thank you," I repeated. I said more. For the first time I said, "Thank you God, for taking care of my son, thank you."

God took care of me that day—and I knew he was taking care of Aaron. After I made my way back to Tiger Bob, I ran to anyone I saw. Like the widow in the Bible who found her missing coin and invited her friends to a party to tell them about her good fortune, I too told them what God did for me.

Sonic, a young female hiker, stood in the middle of the powerline clearing. I'd met her a few days before, she had an impish quality about her. Today she looked like an angel, with her eyes closed, her hands folded across her chest, and her face pointed to the heavens. Christian music played from her iPod.

"Sonic, Sonic, let me tell you what just happened!" I said and told her about Aaron and how I got back my poles.

"I felt the presence of God," I exclaimed with tears in my eyes.

"Well, let me tell you this," she replied. "I stopped here to pray because I felt the presence of angels."

I fell backward. I'd started this hike one hundred and nineteen days earlier. After almost seventeen hundred miles, I ended up on a major ski resort on the anniversary of the death of my son, a ski lift mechanic. To "lose" my fourteen-inch tent poles out of an eight-inch pocket after that distance doesn't make sense. Tiger Bob, right behind me, never saw them fall. We had full view of the trail, and we saw no one else on the trail until I found them. And Sonic, the angelic hiker, told me she stopped at this site because of the presence of angels. I wasn't just snapped back into reality—I was snapped into spirituality.

The probability of all these things happening is staggering. On this day, God showed me he cares about everything in my life—from my tent poles to my son.

Andy, I have a plan, he told me. *You are a part of it, and so is Aaron. Even your tent poles are part of my plan. Today, know I am taking care of you. Just walk, Andy. Walk in faith.*

What started me back on my road to God was when I realized he gave up his son. God is a person—not a human person, but he is a person. He gave us his emotions. God knew his son would die when he sent him to us. God knew his son would die. He showed his displeasure when he darkened the sky. When he tore the temple curtain, he let us know we have a direct path to him. He expressed his love for us and triumphed over death when he arose on the third day. God lost a son. He knows grief, anger, and sadness. God gets me. He is part of my club and he is more.

The second step on my road back to God began with answering the question of where God was on the twenty-seventh. *I was there,* he told me. *I lifted my child Aaron out of the carnage, past his Harley, over the minivan, and now—he is with me.*

The third step happened when I realized God has a plan for me and had one for Aaron. All along the way, he showed me he was in control. Today, he grabbed me by the shirt collar to leave no doubt. My mountaintop experience was a mountaintop miracle.

I asked God for a story, and he gave me one. For the rest of the trail, I told whoever would listen. Some looked at their wristwatches and walked away; others smiled and said someone must be looking out for me. Everyone heard, and everyone had a choice to believe what I believed—God is interested in everything about us. I still had over four hundred miles and two more states before Mt Katahdin in Maine. Just like a marathoner whose race doesn't begin until the last miles, my pilgrimage had just begun.

CHAPTER 13

The Ice Cream Man

I could have gone home. I experienced the inexplicable. I called Lori and told her. She wept, she understood, she believed.

"As far as I know," I told her, "an angel carried my poles from Mt Killington to me." *Did it really matter how?* God was at work.

It was what she waited to hear for four months.

"Keep going," she said, "there's more." She was right. In a twenty-six-mile marathon, the real race begins at mile eighteen. I was at mile eighteen.

Four weeks. One month seemed too long, four hundred miles seemed too far, and two states seemed too many. But four weeks? *I can do four weeks.*

My usual knee joint pain was alive and kicking. The trail was the same root and rock affair I'd followed since Georgia. Tiger pressed to finish, so he could get home for a family reunion. I had no time constraints and relished walking into the White Mountains. I seemed to be holding him back and thought about telling Tiger to go on without me. After stopping at a cabin with an observation deck and eating a chocolate bar, I rejuvenated and finished strong.

We got a short resupply and camped beneath towering pines for our last night in Vermont. In my blog, I recorded:

> Yesterday was exhaustive, and this morning brought the aftershocks. But experiencing the love, prayers, and support from friends and family bolstered my energy and determination to finish with conviction.

WHEN SUNDAY SMILED

I read about grace in the New Testament while being a member of this Appalachian nomadic tribe. Christ talked about grace in the gospels, and Paul encouraged new Christians: both Jews and Gentiles. Grace counted in the wild with strangers, thru-hikers, and just everyone I met. There is no time to be suspicious. Life is just too dang short.

After walking down Thistle Hill, we started across a bridge in West Hartford, Vermont. At the end of the bridge, a woman came out on her porch and rang a bell, beckoning us to come closer. She offered sodas and fruit and invited us into their modest home for breakfast. The husband and wife didn't want to advertise in any trail guides because they liked surprising hikers with their trail magic. When we sat down to a full breakfast of eggs, sausage, and toast, they told us their home had washed away in a hurricane. Several years later, they were still rebuilding but the husband lost his job. Despite having limited funds, they remained committed to feeding hikers.

After walking over the last mountain in Vermont, we stopped for lunch at Happy Hill Shelter, the oldest shelter on the trail. The rebuilt small stone shelter looked like something out of a Grimm's fairy tale. The three sides of stone formed the walls beneath the steep wood-shingled roof. As I sat on its porch eating the last of my sandwich, DuPont, known throughout the hiker network, came barreling down the path. Rumors had him getting kicked out of six trail towns. When sober, DuPont scammed his way along the trail, and when he wasn't, he fought with anyone.

Before he stopped walking, he bellowed, "Hey! Do you guys have any food?"

"Can you at least say hello first?" I replied.

Trail etiquette dictates hikers never ask other thru-hikers for food or water. They are precious, and we are expected to be self-sufficient. We may sit close to a family barbecue and salivate while we wait for leftovers—but we never beg.

Two pairs of jeans and an extra flannel shirt spilled out the sides of his torn backpack. Reputations travel faster than hikers. DuPont had a problem with alcohol, but today he was sober.

"I don't get my check until the end of the month, and I need something to eat," he explained. "I have PTSD."

After being discharged as an Army soldier guarding Germany's border, he worked in a labor union for a few years. Alcohol appeared to be a bigger problem, but we gave him a peanut butter sandwich and an apple before we left the shelter. Some people wave the American flag to gain sympathy, but refusing him food would have been wrong. He needed more than lunch. Jesus said, "Feed my sheep."[6] Today, we fed DuPont, but tomorrow, he was on his own. We gave DuPont lunch, but he was still hungry.

After giving away some food, we hurried down the mountain and onto a street lined with coolers and boxes of food for thru-hikers. We walked across the large stone-arched Ledyard Bridge, which spanned the broad Connecticut River, and into Hanover, New Hampshire, home to Dartmouth College. The historic town had several amenities for hikers including free donuts and pizza.

After checking AWOL's A.T. guide, I found a nearby house who took in hikers. A pair of retired Navy doctors didn't charge hikers but accepted donations to stay at their house. Throughout my hike, I'd stayed in a basement, a barn, a backyard, under a bridge, and now in an RV. The couple put us up in their broken-down RV parked in the driveway and offered access to a shower, laundry, and kitchen.

In less than twenty-four hours, I had three encounters with people leading different lives. Each was on a different path. The first family had little but gave all they could; the second, DuPont, gave nothing, but took all he could; and the third couple had much but still gave what they had.

I wrote:

> I can't believe I am in New Hampshire. I have two states to walk through and my A.T. journey will come to an end. After four months of living life on my feet and from what's on my back, I am not sure how to behave anymore. The path of soft dirt and leaves took us on an easy downhill hike. I used to not like it when the trail took me on regular roads, but now an easy road is a thing of joy.

After we left Hanover, we sped down the mountain dancing from rock to rock. Most days, I couldn't keep up with Tiger on the downhills. He laughed at me as I examined each rock and I held my breath whenever he slipped from going too fast.

Downhills didn't scare me; downhills hurt. I was strong going uphill. In Georgia, I would stop midway to catch my breath, but in New England I didn't stop until I reached the top. Downhill was a different story. The lack of cartilage in my joints made going downhill a test of physical and mental reserve. When I got a jolt of pain, I wondered how much worse my knee would get.

Today, I had fun matching my partner step for step. We caught up to a younger hiker refilling his water bottles.

"You guys really book," he said.

Yeah, for old farts.

We were headed down the mountain for Bill Ackerly's house. Bill was an A.T. icon known as the Ice Cream Man, who advertised "the best water on the trail." He offered sage advice and gave thru-hikers rides and a place to stay. Although early in the morning when we arrived, Bill was taking another hiker to a different trailhead. When he returned, this retired psychiatrist with a whimsical view on life entertained us with ice cream, insight, and water. Inside, Tiger Bob spotted a picture of a lady slipper orchid on Bill's fridge. When Tiger hit his lowest, he often saw a lady slipper, so seeing one in Bill's kitchen meant a lot to him.

"Every time I needed help, the good Lord would put a lady slipper in front of me," he told me. When Tiger Bob saw the lady slipper picture, he knew we were at a special place.

 Despite Bill being an old man, he looked more boy than man. There are people in this world who have a way of making people around them feel good. People liked being around Bill. 2015 was his last year helping hikers—he died the next year, May 23, 2016, eighty-seven-years young.

The White Mountains, the jewel of the Appalachian Trail, beckoned in the distance. The Whites comprise a formidable range above the tree line with horrendous rock scrambles, unpredictable weather, and spectacular views. They are special. After the Whites is the Hundred-Mile Wilderness … and after the Wilderness is Katahdin. I was close and determined to savor the moment. Armed with my strengthened faith, I wanted to walk out of the White Mountains knowing I lived every moment in the moment. I wanted the playful attitude of Bill Ackerly the Ice Cream Man, the generosity of trail angels, and the patience to deal with the DuPonts of this world.

CHAPTER 14

Don't Let Me Quit

Yesterday I ended late, too tired to write an entry in this electronic journal. Today we ended even later, and I am even more tired. Two productive days in terms of mileage, both over twenty miles, but it is not how far you go. Sometimes I hurtle down the mountain, which can be fun, but hurtling can be a distraction from why I am out here.

Mount Moosilauke, the first formidable mountain in the White Mountain chain, stood at 4,802 feet. The mountain was a B-E-A-S-T. The tough, long, and beautiful climb brought me above the tree line. I expected the White Mountains to be a barren slab of granite shimmering in the sunlight. Most of the mountains however, looked like many of the mountains I already climbed, green scrub pine that survived between rocks and a thin layer of soil until the tree line. Above the line, bold rock formations stood on the barren but beautiful wasteland. We climbed over rocks and slipped on roots worn away from countless storms and throngs of hikers on this fragile trail.

What made the White Mountains different lay above the tree line. Trees shrunk as I approached the line of demarcation where mature plant life cannot grow. Once towering over one hundred feet, trees now looked back at us at eye level before being reduced to shrubs. Surrounded by a field of rocks, the steep grade flattened out where even the pine shrubs couldn't survive. After one false summit, I made my way to the next—the top of Moosilauke.

I thought my fears were over, but my anxiety worked on me. I knew I would complete this climb ... I couldn't drop in the middle of the trail. *But, what about tomorrow, and the day after?* When you think you are at the top, the trail just keeps going up. Above the tree line counted for twice as much below. As I got closer to the summit, I got slower. The air was blustery, the sun bright, and in the distance, I saw lighting that made the view more impressive. I was not keeping up with Tiger Bob.

Tucking behind the rocks at the top, I sat on some soft moss to make myself lunch. Exasperated, I called Lori and whispered, "Don't let me quit."

"What?" she asked.

"Don't let me quit!" I cried. Everyone on the summit heard.

"Oh, no! You are so close, you got this ... you got this, babe."

She called me 'babe,' I must really be hurting. I regained my composure. My weakness embarrassed me. I wanted to be strong for Lori, not weak.

In the early days on the trail, I would call her crying, "It's so hard."

The next day I'd call her back crying, "I'm so happy."

She was at home alone, dealing with her grief while taking care of our house and talking to our kids. I confused her. I confused myself. I often got to a summit and shed tears. My tears came from the sheer majesty of the mountains. They also came because in my moments of ecstasy I thought of Aaron, knowing he would never be here to share the moment. My rapid roller coaster of borderline emotions was dizzying.

"I'm such a baby," I said to Tiger. He looked at me perplexed as we headed down the mountain.

As difficult as the trail proved going up Moosilauke, the trail proved worse going down, much worse. For five miles, the trail paralleled water streaming over rocks. I slipped on the steep, treacherous rocks. Tiger was far ahead. The trail used wooden steps and metal bars drilled into the side of rock to make the descent possible. Hordes of day hikers made their way up and down the mountain. Tourists congested the Whites on weekends.

As I got to the bottom, a sign pointed to trail magic for thru-hikers. Exasperated and exhausted, this simple act of kindness restored me. God knew. Two angels from a local trail club cooked up hamburgers and hot dogs. Ramses, who got his name for sleeping with his arms folded across his chest like an Egyptian mummy, walked up to the group with homebaked brownies.

Wolf Mountain, our last climb for the day, lay before us. This desceptive mountain proved to be just as formidable as much taller mountains with its multiple peaks, and tired trail. Weekend hikers already jammed into Elijah Brook Shelter before we arrived. I set up my tent, cooked, and completed my sock washing ritual before retiring for the night. After another arduous day in the White Mountain range, I typed in my blog:

> Today I passed the 400 miles-to-go mark and the 1,800-mile mark. I am not quitting.

Sunday used to be a difficult day for me. Since my day on Mount Killington, Sundays became an increasing source of comfort. Sunday is a day of rest, a day to restore the soul. After nine miles, which included hiking over Kinsman Mountain at 4,358 feet, we got a ride into North Woodstock, New Hampshire, to resupply and regroup. I wanted to cut back the mileage in the Whites to enjoy my hike. I wrote:

> The White Mountains are like no other, and one mile in the Whites is like two miles anywhere else on the trail. So it's time to readjust my expectations, cut my mileage to fifteen miles, not worry about the pace, and take it one day at a time. I don't
>
>
>
> want to worry about the road up ahead like I did when I first started this trek. It could be the terrain, maybe it's getting colder, but regardless, I am determined to focus on today. And today I am restored.

I begged a ride at Franconia Notch from a whitewater outfitter to get to North Woodstock. We got another ride from an energetic grandmother thrilled to pick up a pair of beleaguered hikers. She talked about wanting to do the A.T. and planned to hike the John Muir Trail in California. Her mother sat next to her and her grandson sat in the back next to us as she drove further to drop us off at the hostel.

At the hostel, I laid out my wet tent and dirty clothes in the sun. The exertion of the trail matched with the anxiety of getting to town contributed to my malaise. I was always sleepy in town and wouldn't wake up until I got back to the woods.

The hostel combined everyone's laundry. "We never have had a problem," they claimed. Tiger didn't believe her, and the next day, both of us were missing one sock. My two pairs of Merino wool socks were precious, but I was uncharacteristically gracious. *Maybe I am changing.*

North Woodstock proved to be a good place to get a good meal and ice cream, but the town didn't have what I wanted for my food supplies. After so much time on the trail, my menu was exact. My basic menu did not contain enough calories, so I relied on prepackaged snacks. I looked for energy bars loaded with calories—durable and edible. They pack a small protein punch. I used to turn down candy bars, but a piece of butterscotch or caramel hard candy worked miracles on sweat-soaked climbs up the mountains.

The Whites' hut system became my new source for additional calories. The huts are a series of large rustic cabins with a few rooms of multiple bunk beds, sometimes stacked three to the ceiling. A large dining room, commercial kitchen, compost toilets, and showers completed the rustic niche. Section-hikers paid a premium for such amenities, but thru-hikers got the leftovers of cold oatmeal and pancakes after breakfast and warm soup after lunch.

My nights got colder. The month was August, but August in New England isn't August in the North Carolina Outer Banks. I still had the same sleeping system I started with: my forty-degree quilt along with my nylon bivvy sack and silk liner. Most hikers carried a heavier bag at the beginning and switched them for a lighter bag after the Smokies, then got their heavier gear back in New Hampshire. When I got back on the trail in New Jersey, I brought back my long underwear and Gore-Tex gloves but kept my same sleeping bag.

The weather in the Whites is notorious. The fickle weather snows somewhere every month in this mountain chain. I live in North Carolina and hiked with a guy from South Carolina—we valued warm and dry. We were on constant alert for weather fronts.

Epic is one word in a hiker's vocabulary that gets overused. A bear encounter could be epic; a sunset, epic. A cheeseburger and beer at the right time was epic. In the White Mountains, I used the word "epic." They were. Never again would I experience such mountaintops—they were epic.

Never again would I experience such dramatic weather—it was epic. Hikers have a limited vocabulary, but epic could not be overused for the Whites.

The word "nice," however, was another overused trail word.

"Where are you from?" someone would ask.

"Outside of Philadelphia," I'd reply, and then wait for the expected response.

"Nice."

"Oh, have you been there?" I'd ask. "Nice."

Someone would ask, "How far did you hike today?"

"Nice."

"Eating noodles?"

"Nice."

"Going to the privy?"

You get the idea. Everything was nice. Hikers are mellow, which made life nice on the trail. The end of the day was nice. Sometimes, the trail was gritty. Sometimes, I just wanted to go home, but in the end, the trail was nice.

It thundered after an epic day of hiking Little Haystack Mountain, Mount Lafayette, Mount Lincoln, and Mount Garfield. Thunder anywhere else meant keep walking. Thunder in the middle of the New Hampshire White Mountains meant run fast. Section-hikers, out for a few days, scurried to the top to avoid the imminent rain. One young woman told her boyfriend to go ahead without her. I caught him at the top and suggested he should wait for his girlfriend.

"But she told me to keep going," he said and walked into the dry hut.

"I guess chivalry is dead," I remarked, and thought about when Aaron opened his sister's door and told her, "Chivalry is not dead, Ali, unless you let it die."

Aaron's cowboy-time-honored traditions honored women. I didn't want chivalry to die either. I wanted that strength. I didn't want to sit on a mountaintop crying, "Don't let me quit." I longed for the quiet confidence of a cowboy.

We ducked into Galehead Hut, a summer camp for the rich kids who never grew up. The White Mountains' hut system is for outdoorsy people from New York City. They paid a hundred and fifty bucks or more to scratch their back-to-nature itch. Nice. The huts had no hot water, no flush toilets, and everyone slept in bunk beds. Patrons got a great dinner and breakfast, and we got the leftovers. They never turned away thru-hikers when the weather turned nasty.

We stopped for a bowl of soup when the clouds opened, and the rain came down in, yes, *epic* proportions. When the rain, thunder, and lightning picked up, the manager explained the tradition of "work-for-stay." As thru-hikers, he told us we could have the leftovers from dinner and sleep on the floor if we worked an hour in the kitchen.

"You had me at leftovers." Later I confided, "I used to work at the Anderson House: Home of Gracious Dining as a bus boy and dish washer." They weren't impressed.

Like dutiful servants, Tiger and I grinned when a girl showed us how to set the table with forks on the left, knives pointed inward, and no napkins. After watching the section-hikers have their fill, which took forever, the staff gave us a medley of soup, vegetables, and bruschetta. To my amazement, Captain K, the eccentric pilot, was in the kitchen. He and I scraped the frost from the inside of the freezer. We asked for more work, so we cleaned the thick grease from the stove. I didn't ask again.

I even had cell phone service, so I called back to the hostel to tell them I found my Merino sock in the pocket of my jacket. I called Lori telling her how well we were doing, and that I wanted to be strong for her. Her confidence grew when she heard about my progress.

The thunder and lightning show looked ominous as I watched from a dry secure building. Ecstatic to be taken care of again, I unrolled my down quilt and fell asleep on the dining room floor, confident in my world and God. The hut system showed mercy on me surrounded by the grandeur of God's creation. I hiked during perilous times and lived in the moment.

After we left the security of Galehead Hut in the morning, we saw signs at an intersection. The signs looked like crosses marking the trail. We rushed right by them thinking we knew where to go before backtracking a half mile up the mountain.

"We can't do that again," said Tiger Bob, but we would.

The White Mountains have lots of different trails leading up to each summit to accommodate hordes of hikers, and lots of signs, but the A.T. white blazes were absent. I didn't want to walk twenty-mile days in the Whites, but that's what we did to make up for the short mileage from the day before.

"I thought you weren't going to walk that far?" Lori questioned when I called her from a mountain top. But I did, and my muscles were fatigued.

We stopped at Zealand Falls Hut where we scarfed up the last of the cold scrambled eggs, oatmeal, and lukewarm coffee. A worker at the hut asked me to deliver a letter to Carter Notch Hut and scribbled out a message on a piece of cardboard.  The hut workers are college students who form a tight group and work long hours at minimal pay. They often return the next year because of their love of the mountains and the camaraderie. These young people hoisted wooden-framed packs to hike in all the needed supplies and hike out what little refuse they collect. To keep up their morale, they sent each other messages via thru-hikers.

I took my responsibility as seriously as any dedicated postal worker. I stowed the improvised envelope in an inside pocket in my pack and figured my mission would take two days.

The sun had long set when we finished climbing Mount Webster and Mount Jackson in the middle of the Presidential Mountain chain. The temperature dropped, and the wind blew hard telling us to get off the summit.

President Jackson, renowned for his toughness, once shot a man in a duel. His mountain proved to be just as formidable. After walking over twenty miles, we showed up at Mitzpah Hut. Some other hikers had already taken the work-for-stay option at the crowded hut.

At Mitzpah Hut, I spied Funk, the hiker who, along with Just Greg, hiked with me in Georgia and Tennessee. I caught up to him after four months of hiking and two weeks of zeroes. Funk hiked strong, but he enjoyed the comforts of a warm hostel and a soft bed. Thrilled to see someone from my original group, I asked him to join us. Funk now hiked shorter mileage at a more genteel pace in contrast to his original pace line when I couldn't keep up with him climbing up the Georgia mountains. He declined my offer.

At our site, I dried out my tent, made dinner, and had just enough light to set up on a wooden platform. The platforms were built on uneven ground to minimize the imprint while creating more space. Two backpacking tents could fit on one platform. Tiger improvised by using his hiking pole to stretch the back of his tarp to the floor. At 1:30 in the morning, I woke to the sound of rain and recorded:

> … yet I know I am dry, warm, and safe. My thoughts dwell on the interactions of the day, my life back home, and getting through another day with enough of what I need to rise above my circumstances. When it gets light, I will again pack up my wet tent and head for Mt. Washington, the tallest of the Presidentials. I hope to walk fifteen and end at a reasonable time; I don't want to tempt fate. Already we have been pushing too hard. That has resulted in falling more than once, slipping often, and straining joints and ligaments to exhaustion.

If the White Mountains are the "Jewel of the Appalachian Trail," then Mount Washington, at 6,288 feet, is the crown jewel. Washington is renowned for having the worst weather in the contiguous United States. The fog moved in, but we moved on anyway toward the tallest presidential mountain by way of Eisenhower, Franklin, and Monroe. *More presidents, more mountains.* I struggled onward with an eye towards the clouds. The weather got worse as the temperature dropped, and the mist grew stronger. Mount Washington is quite the attraction, including a narrow-gauge cog train for tourists. The commercialized mountain came complete with a snack bar and museum. The worst weather spot in the United States sold souvenirs. Tourists looked incredulous when we explained we'd walked from Georgia before they got back on their train, and we got on our way.

The weather turned to rain and brief hail. I surged forward, taking on the rock field as a challenge. Tiger Bob remarked about my speed up the next peaks of Jefferson and Madison. *Davidsons are mudders.* As time moved away from July twenty-seventh, my burden lessened. I got stronger. Grief is not just in the head; grief takes over the whole body affecting the endocrine system. The glands secrete adrenaline and cortisol under stress. I blogged:

> As I shed the intense feelings with matching hormones, I am getting stronger. I still fight back the tears at the summits and lose, but I am strengthening through your prayers.

Despite wearing gloves, a rain jacket to block the wind, shorts, and a ski cap, when I stopped, I shivered and stiffened as the weather deteriorated. I'd learned to hike in the rain in shorts and synthetic T-shirt, but now the chill factor told me to don an extra layer.

Today the wind talked, and I listened. I struggled to put on my rain jacket in the constant wind. Walking between the rocks sounded like a wind tunnel. We stopped at the next hut, Madison Spring Hut, and offered our services for work-for-stay. The manager told us we were too early. I told him the irony of walking over twenty miles the day before when we were too late for work-for-stay. He was a Wake Forest alum, so he and Tiger Bob, a Clemson alum, did the secret ACC handshake, and he granted us our last work-for-stay. Cold and wet is a recipe ripe for hypothermia, so we bivouacked inside a warm building with leftovers. After a twenty-plus mile day yesterday, I wiped windows and tables underneath a dry roof.

> The trail has been a humbling experience for me. When I first started this venture, I wanted above all to finish, so I could say with pride I am a thru-hiker, something few can say. However, I now know if I finish it will be from a point of humility and not pride. I can't do this without the generosity of friends, family, fellow hikers, and strangers. Today a total stranger gave me a lighter to light my stove, the manager gave me a dry roof and warm food, and countless others offered their encouragement. I am humbled as a child of God, a man, and a thru-hiker. It is still raining as I write these thoughts with the din of hut guests dining in the background. Did I mention how thrilled I am?

With reluctance, we left the warm, dry confines of the hut the next day into the swirling winds of Mount Madison for our worst hiking weather in the Whites. This mountain chain would not let us go without a signature battle. My pack cover acted like a parachute as we climbed over huge boulders into crosswinds measuring up to forty-plus miles per hour. The wind almost blew me off the trail. I secured my tablet/camera in my pack and did not take a picture all day but forever etched in my mind. My knees screamed for relief, but until we got below the tree line, there would be no relief. Once among the pines, the world returned to normal. The scene was from *Paradise Lost* when the travelers in a wintery blizzard stumbled through the rocks to peaceful Shangri-La. No snow, but the wind proved *epic.*

After the wind blizzard, we bounded down the trail thinking we would be at the bottom of the mountain before noon. But we passed by another trail sign without reading it, adding eight more miles to the journey downward to the Appalachian Mountain Club (AMC) at Pinkham Notch. Tiger and I argued about which way to go until we backtracked four miles to find the sign. Its writing was on the opposite side of the direction we hiked, so we never saw the sign the first time.

AAAAAHHH! I thought we wouldn't make that mistake again! Bob was anxious to get to the bottom where his older sister was waiting to hike with us. Trudy patiently waited for us to arrive at the Appalachian Mountain Club headquarters and alas, greeted us with a picnic lunch in the afternoon, although we were weary beyond belief.

The Appalachian Mountain Club differs from the Appalachian Trail Conservancy. It maintains the trail and hut system in New Hampshire while the A.T.C maintains the entire Appalachian Trail. The A.T. uses the same trails as the AMC. The AMC focused on its many side trails catering to the many day hikers.

The White Mountains are a mecca for hikers from around the world. Multiple accents and languages surrounded us. Despite the bright sun, the gentle breeze put a crisp in the air. Summer in New England felt more like spring because we had just come through winter in the Whites. As we recounted the day to Trudy, she got excited about hiking. We planned to hike further that day, but because of the navigational faux pas, we used the time to resupply, clean up, and rest up for another day. Trudy's cabin and a converted barn stood beside a beautiful pond. After one long day, we went from *Paradise Lost* to *On Golden Pond.*

The next day the three of us hiked up the four Wildcat Mountain peaks.

"We're going hiking!" Trudy sang.

Tiger's sister hiked strong up the steep and rocky assent. She pointed out the plants and colors of the mountains reminding us how special they are and how fortunate we were among them. Trudy packed a day-pack with sandwiches and chips. I grew quiet and sat apart when we stopped for a break at another ski mountain. Her plan was to take the gondola down the mountain, but we were early, so she hiked further. We came upon a spring where we broke out the sandwiches then said goodbye to Trudy.

We hiked further to Carter Notch where I delivered the trail mail letter from the Zealand Falls Hut. The cardboard letter took over two days to deliver to a hut less than forty miles away. I was the Pony Express—without the pony or the express. The worker at the other end gave us coffee cake for the effort, totally worth it.

I estimated hiking seven more miles over the Carter Mountain peaks would get us to Imp Campsite by 4:30, but we arrived closer to 6:00. The Whites are measured in mountains. Effort wasn't measured in miles; effort was measured in time. A full day was a full day regardless of how far we traveled.

> I am now tucked in my sleeping bag on a chilly August New England night. Cold I like, but I am always uneasy when I get to camp and shiver. Tomorrow, I will be out of White Mountains Park and away from the hut system I love. I will still have a lot of climbing as the mountains continue into southern Maine and more shivering.

CHAPTER 15

IT'S THE JOURNEY, MAN

I loved the Whites. I loved being out of them. There were more mountains and more challenges, and the desire to be done. I missed my wife. I missed my life, whatever might become of it. I walked farther than I ever thought and lived in the wild longer than I ever did before. The trail gave me an unbounded confidence and the time to think about what I wanted to do once I got off the trail. I didn't want to go back and just get a J.O.B. (just over broke). If I took a J.O.B., my goal would be to quit. I'd work hard, but my goals have changed. Rather than living to work, I would work to live.

I wanted to live my life to the fullest. I had several ideas ranging from starting a hostel in Duncannon, Pennsylvania; to going to a wooden boat building school; to becoming a missionary in Africa. I still had a case of wanderlust and wanted to get in my truck with Lori and Belle to relive our back-packing trips from our twenties when we stopped at National Parks out West.

The change in terrain coincided with my change in temperament. I became something of an extrovert on the trail. Throughout the day, I looked forward to seeing others. My blog reminded me to keep smiling at the trees, to trust others, and to let go of the needless worries. Trusting others would be tough, but through my newfound confidence, if I changed my outlook on life, then I would change my inward depression. In my journal I wrote:

I grew from 'forgettable' to 'Phantom.' I am quick to start a conversation, smile, and say an encouraging word to a fledgling hiker. That's new for me: I trust strangers, I talk to young and old, and I let my initial judgments evaporate like fog filtering through the pines. I still can be bitter, envious, and petty, but not much. I try not to waste time with guilt, doubt, and all the crap that will never change. I'm not a quitter, never was, so it's time to stop thinking like one. Tomorrow I walk into Maine; that's what I need to do—just walk.

I was intent to approach the last state with my improved outlook on life and others. Tiger Bob and I camped at Gentian Pond, ten miles away from Mahoosuc Notch. The next day, we walked ten miles over Mount Success and Goose Eye Mountain peaks before getting to the most difficult and fun mile of the trail. The rock formation is a veritable amusement park for the back-packer. A valley of huge boulders piled on top of each other formed a natural maze. I took off my pack and shoved it forward through small tunnels between the rocks. Then I climbed to the top of more boulders—sometimes twenty feet in the air and jumped from one rock to the next.

I grabbed the top of a young tree to rappel down the side of a boulder. The thin tree bent over as I made my way to the ground. Part way down, I slipped against the rock but got down unscathed and still smiling. The notch seemed further than just a mile. I wore myself out jumping, climbing, and crawling through the maze. When I thought I was nearing the end, there were more rocks to conquer.

"Just like life," I joked with a couple going the other way. They laughed and kept going.

At the end of the notch, I met two hikers who weren't laughing. They'd guessed wrong and fallen off the rocks. The notch left them cut and bruised, a testament to how serious this natural amusement park could be.

I handled Mahoosuc Notch, but I wasn't prepared for the climb up Mahoosuc Arm. Mahoosuc Arm rose over fifteen-hundred feet in one-and-a-half miles. With each step I repeated, "God is good, God give me strength, God is good, God give me strength." My mantra helped me relax my breathing and settle into a hypnotic-like state. I didn't have to think; I trusted. I didn't hide my exhaustion when I called Lori at the top. She noticed the strain in my voice, but this time I assured her I was fine.

"I'm tired, but I'm on top and past the toughest mile of the Appalachian Trail," I told her. The climb drained most of the energy from my muscles, but my inner resolve was secure.

I dropped down to the campsite at Speck Pond long after Tiger Bob at 6:00 p.m. Darkness settled in by the time I set up my tent, got water, and made dinner. After crawling into my tent before shutting my eyes in the great state of Maine, I read a verse that summed up the day. "Indeed, we felt that we had received the sentence of death. But that was to make us rely not on ourselves but on God who raises the dead."[7]

I may have been out of the White Mountain chain, but I wasn't out of the mountains. Southern Maine could be just as tough as anywhere on the trail, but at least the trail was well-marked. The people of Maine took pride in the trail. The state has few people, few cities, but miles of wilderness. Yet, they maintained the trail by building rock steps and sometimes moving the path to avoid erosion. The signs were neat, similar, and well-placed. I continued to climb mountains with outstanding views, and I walked around countless lakes and meadows. Small towns dotted the trail populated with friendly people. The variety of the Maine wilderness changed daily.

After hiking over the pair of Baldpate peaks, we headed into the hamlet of Andover for resupply. The Pine Ellis Hostel served hikers at the bottom of the mountain. The converted house was an old two-story farmhouse with a porch the width of the front. We had a room to ourselves, and the beds were layered with quilts. Andover is defined by one intersection, which caters to thru-hikers and snowmobilers. We got resupplied at the hostel and had dinner at the General Store.

I talked to Tiger Bob at dinner about splitting up our partnership. Tiger's deadline to be home for a family reunion pushed him to put in additional miles. I had no deadline and wanted to slow down to enjoy the last state. Our quest would soon be over, so he wanted us to stick together. Although he listened to me, he didn't quite understand the pressure I felt to keep up with him. I didn't like the thought of holding him back. I decided to stick with him.

How I got to this point was a mystery. My general plan was to be here in August and here I was, right on "schedule" without having a schedule, just a goal. Tiger and others mapped each day out and constantly reshuffled their numbers because each day produced the unexpected. I gave up on my twenty-mile-per-day schedule in Tennessee when I came back from the trial in Colorado.

I know I walked here, my feet told me so. One day I was on a Greyhound bus, the next day I was in our hometown of Duncannon, Pennsylvania, and now, over four months later, I was in Maine. I took in the beauty, including the little towns that defined the state as much as the ponds.

I wanted to take a zero in Andover, the forecast called for rain and lots of it, but Tiger convinced me to head out with him the next day. In the morning, I woke up sobbing, still wondering why God didn't put his hand in front of Aaron's motorcycle instead of a Chrysler minivan. When grief comes, it never completely goes away. Later, I asked Tiger if he heard me sobbing, and he just nodded. As I put my feet on the floor, my thoughts subsided, my faith became clearer, comforted in part that God put his hand under Aaron and lifted him home. I will have to wait for a more complete answer if there is such a thing. *Does why really matter? I mean, what would why change?*

The day started well with a hearty breakfast back at the General Store and a 7:00 a.m. shuttle to the trailhead. The path was to my liking with a challenging uphill to warm up my legs as Tiger headed out ahead of me. I hiked alone up and over Old Blue Mountain in a mild drizzle. The sky was grey, and the report of a storm front proved likely as the morning moved on, and so did I.

When I slipped on the trail, I felt the hand of God was on my back to catch me before I fell. I still fell sometimes, but I felt his presence, and I was not afraid.

The graceful pines caught the gentle rain and kept me dry until twenty yards from Bemis Mountain Lean-to. The rain let loose. Shelters in Maine are called lean-tos and are similar in size and location. The three-sided lean-tos held eight people and were close to water and the trail. We hiked only six miles, we were making great time, I was healthy, and we were under cover with dry feet. The thought of hiking out in a cold rain kept us inside the dry shelter, free from hypothermia.

Several other hikers showed up throughout the day. A young science teacher was first. He rigged his iPod speaker inside his cooking pot and hung his contraption overhead, which increased the volume of Johnny Cash above the rain on the metal roof. A father and his three teenage daughters showed up later in their rain gear. The dad said their family had hiked since his children were small. The girls laughed as they told stories. After watching the rain for an hour, they danced like fairies down the trail to meet their mother at the road. They never complained once about the weather.

I wrote:

> They all seem content, so I will take their lead. I am in my sleeping bag getting the rest of a zero day I was thinking about taking anyway—still feeling the hand of God.

The rain cleared the next day, leaving a series of puddles in place of the trail. Halfway into the hike, I gave up dodging the water to keep my feet dry and dove in feet first. I was liberated after I accept my fate, no longer living in fear of soggy boots. I forded three deep creeks. At first, I took off my shoes and wore my thrift store water socks. Later, I plowed forward across the swift creeks to clean the mud out of my dirty hiking shoes while Tiger Bob hiked ahead.

Monk, an older hiker who section-hiked at a leisurely pace was at the next shelter. He told me Tiger would be camping alongside the creek about five miles down the trail. When I pulled out my map, I realized I'd dropped my reading glasses along the trail.

"There's a pair of glasses in the shelter," Monk said.

As I picked them up, I noticed they weren't just store-bought reading glasses but were military prescription. My exact prescription.

Monk mentioned a woman had disappeared from this shelter in 2013. Geraldine Largay, a sixty-six-year-old hiker got off the trail in search of water and was lost for almost a month before dying of starvation. Her body was found two years later, less than a half mile from the trail with her trail journal lying next to her.

I could no longer keep up with Tiger and planned to tell him when I caught up with him at our next campsite. The time was already 5:30 when I got to the stream. From talking to other hikers, they told me someone with an orange shirt and Clemson handkerchief tied to the back of his pack had hiked further. Too tired to catch him, I tented along the rapid creek and tried to text him. The short rain day meant my resupply schedule needed revamping. I sent Tiger another text hoping he had phone service and assumed I was now on my own in Maine.

It will work out, God cares, remember? I told myself.

WHEN SUNDAY SMILED

The next day started in typical fashion with my knees talking to each other. That morning my left ankle weighed in on the conversation, *what about me, I have two screws?* I'd broken my ankle when I fell out of our  barn several years ago. I still wondered if a sudden turn or slip would end it all now that I was so close to the end. Several hikers commented on the same paranoia and became superstitious when crossing rocks and roots. I began repeating, "Hand of God, hand of God," as I made my way down the rocks.

My body quieted down, and I hiked past some gorgeous water. Maine is blessed with an abundance of lakes, streams, and rivers, and best of all, the water wasn't puddled in front of me on the trail. I hiked around a large lake marked by a single red cottage. *Who was his high school guidance counselor?* I wondered.

On the way to Rangeley, I slowed down to take in the details of the trees and surrounding greens. I stopped to touch the textures, to smell the forest, and I stopped to pray. I sat by two old canoes for lunch along a picturesque lake. A southbound section-hiker stopped for water but left in a hurried manner missing the moment.

At the road, I ran into Lavender, who I had not seen since Pennsylvania. She lamented she was off the trail but was driving to support her husband, who was going at a quicker pace. She recommended I go to the Farmhouse Hostel and gave me a ride. I scored a private room for the cost of the bunk house and rode into town to pick up more supplies. I could have stretched out my provisions, but now I would slow down, starting in Rangeley.

The Farmhouse Hostel is a large home from the late 1800s, which was being renovated by the owners using reclaimed lumber and beams. Even more special was the family-like atmosphere with kids of all ages running around the yard and doing chores. The farm felt like our farm in Pennsylvania as the family worked together throughout the day. The farmhouse even boasted a pet potbelly pig.

In the evening, as I sat by my tablet computer, a young Ridgerunner, Grace, came in with her banjo and sang a set of lyrical bluegrass songs.

The room was dark, dimly lit by the fire. Music along the trail is special. I harkened back to the Smokies when Six Strings played his ukulele four months ago in Tennessee. The next day, I talked with the owner and told her how much I appreciated seeing her husband and son working together. She understood when I told her about my kids and to remember the moment.

The morning got off to a casual start after a breakfast befitting a selfie. I found a pair of sunglasses on my way to the top of Saddleback and Saddleback Junior, so I hung them on my pack. At the top of Saddleback, the grateful owner found me and gave me a Snickers Bar for the return of his prescription glasses. I saw the chance to tell him about losing my glasses and tent poles, but he and his companion seemed skeptical.

After I left for Saddleback Junior, I met the musician from the previous night. By day, Grace was a botanist employed by the A.T.C as a Ridgerunner to educate people on the trail. She pointed out an arctic shrub, likely deposited on Lone Mountain during the ice age.

A waterfall provided the perfect backdrop at the end of the day. My site was an odd spot on a side trail and with a little creativity, it became home. I had to tuck my tent between some roots to fit, but the location was mine. All I heard was the sound of rushing water.

I wrote:

> I think it is the best spot yet. Alone, off the trail, so what if it's a bit canted? And so what if it rains and I become part of the waterfall? Yeah, so what? It's my best spot yet. I just wish I had someone to share it.

When I hiked out in the morning, I needed to make nineteen miles to get to Stafford. I needed to get a little rubber washer for my leaking water filter. A simple thing like a rubber washer stood between me and giardia or some other waterborne disease before I summited the three peaks of Lone, Spaulding, and Crocker mountains.

AWOL's trail guide showed the elevation with a simple line silhouetting the mountains with coinciding numbers. Today's elevations looked doable on paper but proved formidable on the hard (a sailing term for land). I would not get to the road before 7:00 p.m. and thought about camping along the road, then going into town the next day. My legs were heavy; my heart was just not in it.

WHEN SUNDAY SMILED

As I crested the last peak and headed down the mountain, I met a cute young couple I thought to be from West Virginia due to their accents. I never got accents right, but I kept trying. The guy told me about a "Stay-In-Town-For-Free" card posted at the bottom of the trail. I hustled down the hill and found a small business card stuck to a tree. I wouldn't have seen the little card if I hadn't taken the time to talk to the couple.

After calling the number, a young south-bounder from Indiana named Nat, short for Nat-Geo, came out to pick me up. He was into photography, so we stopped along the road to get a picture of the sunset beyond the lake. We drove to a log cabin owned by Tom, a retired Coast Guard Warrant Officer who was hosting Nat and Happy Warrior, a retired Marine. Being friendly on the trail resulted in some special trail magic.

Happy had stayed at the house for almost a week due to an intestinal virus, and Nat was there for several days. Tom, the owner, was an all-around great guy and offered to let me take a zero. My legs were wearied from the late hike, and I had the time. I found a little slice of heaven outside of Stratton. After taking Sunday off, I gained extra strength for my final assault.

Mount Bigelow and the Hundred-Mile Wilderness stood between me and Mount Katahdin. Tom pointed out Mount Katahdin looming in the distance.

Wow, I'm almost there. Taking a zero put me in line to finish my hike on August 30—Aaron's birthday. I knew I could be on the trail on his birthday when I began hiking, but I couldn't have planned ending on his day. That amount of scheduling would have distracted me from the journey. After two thousand miles and almost five months, somehow, I could end up at the top of Katahdin on that special day. I crossed the two-thousand-mile mark in one calendar year with only 188 miles to go. I was so close to becoming a thru-hiker.

Sunday went by with me relaxing on the upper porch of the log cabin. Tomorrow, I'd say goodbye to one of the trail's best kept secrets. Tom came out on the porch and offered to pick me up at the end of the day and bring me back to his house. Then he would drive me the next day to the trailhead. I just laughed. I said, "Yes, of course. Yes." Tom is another unsung hero of the trail who takes his role as a trail angel to a whole other level. He never advertises, except with a little atay-in-town-for-free-card on a darkened tree.

After my Sunday off, I hiked the Bigelow Mountain chain. From a distance, the Bigelow's looked imposing, but my legs felt great for the first time in months. The climbs were realistic, pleasurable even. I met several hikers, including a young hiker who was contemplating pastoral counseling as a profession and may have needed some of his own. When he found out I was a psychologist, he talked at length about his stepfather intruding on his plans to summit Katahdin. Then he told me he was short on food and asked me for some of my Nutella. I offered him some oatmeal for the next day, but he said he wasn't a big fan of oatmeal and decided to stay at the next lean-to.

Tom, the latest trail angel to save me, drove miles along a dirt road to pick me up and bring me back to his house for one last night. I carried a full pack, which was important, because I didn't slack-pack any portion of the trail and didn't want to start now … I was so close. Being back at Tom's house for one last night was nice. He and Happy Warrior were family. Nat left to start his long walk south. We ate the last of the ribs and homemade pie before his dog licked the last off the plates.

There were several awesome angels named Tom beginning with Tom at Extreme Outfitters, my brother Tom and his son Luke, who got me at the Delaware Water Gap and took me back. And Tom the Senior Chief who agreed to take me from a truck stop to Trail Days, then brought me back to the trailhead hours away the next day. All amazing folks.

After leaving trail angel Tom, Happy Warrior and I hiked for seventeen miles. Happy was a forty-something former Marine whose smile wouldn't quit. Happy Warrior liked to talk, and I didn't mind listening.

My pace was steady, my mind clear, and my legs strong. There are days when the sun is shining, and its rays are created just for me. There are days when the trail unfolds to reveal a soft mat, and even that soft mat appears to be there for me. On this day, I experienced such a day when the world enveloped me in a natural cocoon that sheltered me from all worry or care. I knew I had been this happy in the past, but I couldn't remember when I was so content.

I asked Happy to take my picture to capture my feelings; but alas, the photo did not materialize. The day had to end. I erected my tent ten feet from a lake's edge, close to a small waterfall, as the sun disappeared behind the tree line. The swooning sun created a mirror on the water that echoed the colors of the sky. Earlier two loons called to each other on a pond we circumscribed, and I hoped for a third.

I wrote:

> I am ready for this hike to end, but not tonight. I am sleeping under the stars, and the loons are calling.

In the morning, I hiked a quarter mile to a campground, which piled apple, blueberry, and raspberry pancakes on my plate. The uneven floors and taxidermy overhead amplified the ambiance of the log cabin.

It was a short hike to the Kennebec River where the A.T.C has a canoe to ferry hikers. The ferry operator, Hillbilly Dave, who looked the part, explained the ferry service predated the trail. Even Earl Shaffer, the first thru-hiker, used a canoe service to get across the river. As we crossed the river, I wondered what Shaffer must have felt knowing he hiked over two thousand miles and could see Mt Katahdin in the distance.

The canoe had a white blaze painted on the bottom to make the conveyance part of the official trail. At the top of the road, Hillbilly Dave's wife sat on a tailgate selling drinks and small supplies. I had to tell her how much I appreciated her husband's company, albeit short, before hitching a ride to the Northern Outdoors Center (NOC) to pick up a few supplies.

Happy arrived at the NOC's lodge ahead of me and asked me to stay. I glanced at the restaurant and opted for hot water and a cooked meal. Like the call of the sirens who lured Jason and the Argonauts, or the poppies that lured the lion, scarecrow, and tin man, the hot tub called my name. I took a shower, jumped in the pool, and slid into the hot tub twice more before eating steak and bedding down for the night.

The next day, I dropped a makeshift birthday card for Lori in a mailbox before setting out alone. She would be alone on her birthday. I knew Ali and Robby would call her, but she would be saddened knowing that Aaron would never call again. She would focus on the positive and force a better mood. Lori has told me how vulnerable she is, and I have told her how much stronger than me she really is. Both are true.

I started the route to Monson, the last resupply before the Hundred-Mile Wilderness, without Happy Warrior, when Captain K, the eccentric pilot, passed me. He barely slowed down to tell me he had been off the trail for eight days. Captain K had been popping up since Virginia, but he surprised me every time. And every time, he seemed different. Sometimes he was overly friendly, this time he was oddly brusque.

I'd found another incredible solo camping spot within earshot of a brook when Happy Warrior caught up with me. He was going to zero at the NOC because of the weather but changed his mind. The consummate extrovert, he squeezed his tent onto my solo site. His tent lines crossed over mine. I had to climb on a boulder to make room for my dinner. We made our arrangement work, and he didn't complain about my snoring.

The next day, a gentle mist surrounded me as I made my breakfast fare of oatmeal with Pop-Tart chasers before leaving by 6:15 a.m. The mist turned into rain, which fell to the ground when the wind shook the leaves. I crossed several PUDs (pointless ups and downs), which never really are, along a rapid but shallow stream. In the past, I'd ruminated about pointless past conversations that never needed fixing. Today, I fixated on what I cared about most:

> I care about the weather—right now. Not the weather five days or five minutes ago or five counties away. I care about dry feet—and when they are wet, it's one less thing to care about. I don't care about spelling much, and grammar just a little more. I care about being heard. And when my point is missed, I care a lot. I care about food. Food tastes even better when you can't reach into your fridge or drive around the corner to the Super. I care about my family, I care about the hiker walking towards me. I care about today. I care I have 101 miles to go. When I get my first good view of Mt Katahdin, I will stop caring about the miles, the time, or the effort. I will care about the moment.

I started out before Happy, determined to go at my own pace, on my own schedule. Happy Warrior caught up after a few hours and together we forded a stream holding onto a rope that spanned the water, and then hiked seventeen miles more. We arrived in Monson in the dreary weather and shared a room at the Lakeshore House. Happy became good company, always smiling, always wanting to talk. The forecast called for rain for the next three days, so I stayed in town another day.

WHEN SUNDAY SMILED

The next day, Happy called a section-hiker he'd befriended along the trail to zero at his house for two days due to the weather report. I planned to be through the Wilderness in six days and carry all my supplies. To do this, I could walk less than twenty miles a day. The terrain did not appear formidable on paper after the initial mountain peaks. It never does.

After walking to Shaw's Hostel for their famed all-you-can-eat breakfast, I splurged on a variety of prepackaged Mountain House meals for my final foray. The entire trail, I'd dined on Dollar Store Knorr's noodles and tuna. I was always a bit envious of other hikers whose seven-dollar freeze-dried lasagna made me drool, yet I never tired of my tuna and noodles. More than food, I was looking forward to getting a good look at Mount Katahdin along the trail. That morning, I talked about my travels with a couple who were on vacation. I was doing something they longed to do but likely never would.

Poet, a previous thru-hiker and now owner of Shaw's Hostel, reminded me, "It's not the destination; it's the journey."

He and his wife were teachers in Florida before doing their thru-hike and buying the hostel. That's what the trail does; it shows people they have the courage to follow their dreams. The trail teaches them all things are possible and that it's not the destination, it's the journey.

Monson is a quiet town. Several of the large wooden houses that lined the streets were up for sale. Main Street boasts several churches and abandoned businesses. A lake backs up to the buildings where kayaks, pontoon boats, and fishing holes dot the edge.

After visiting the convenience store twice, Pete's Bakery twice, and the historical society museum once, I was ready for Baxter State Park and ready to go home. But I hadn't faced the Hundred-Mile Wilderness—the last milestone before Katahdin. I could not get enough rest as I was about face the most difficult day during my entire hike.

CHAPTER 16

SUNDAY SMILED

Happy Warrior jumped out of an SUV with a huge smile while I stood at the trailhead. He'd changed his mind again and decided to get back on the trail a day earlier than planned. The entrance to the Hundred-Mile Wilderness was guarded by its large ominous sign:

> THERE ARE NO PLACES TO GET SUPPLIES OR GET HELP UNTIL ABOL BRIDGE ONE HUNDRED MILES NORTH. DO NOT ATTEMPT THIS SECTION UNLESS YOU HAVE AT LEAST TEN DAYS OF FOOD AND ARE FULLY EQUIPPED. THIS IS THE LONGEST WILDERNESS SECTION ON THE ENTIRE APPALACHIAN TRAIL AND ITS DIFFICULTY SHOULD NOT BE UNDERESTIMATED. GOOD HIKING!

"Good Hiking" made me smile. Stories abounded on the trail regarding the Wilderness. Ever since I met South Bounders, I heard tales of horror and feats of strength originating in this vast land. I heard about bogs so deep they could swallow a hiker. Two older hikers told me the trail was not marked, and they carried four weeks of food.

"Four weeks?" I questioned. "That means they planned on averaging about three and a half miles a day."

I met a pair of younger hikers who told me they took three weeks to get through the Wilderness. They contracted trench foot in the wet conditions and had to get off the trail for over a week.

Wilderness? What have we been walking in for the last two thousand miles? Wasn't that wilderness? The tales made me skeptical. A quick look at the map showed a few climbs for the first half of the wilderness before the trail flattened. I could do the wilderness in five days if I walked twenty miles a day. I packed six days of food and planned to average sixteen to seventeen miles a day. *The wilderness is just more trees, more rocks, roots, and more mud. I can do this.* But I hadn't seen a warning sign before, so I prayed before stepping into the forest. I switched my hiking shoes for my four-dollar water socks to make my way across the first stream and held onto a rope overhead for balance.

Toward the end of the day, I saw a sign pointing to trail magic down an old dirt road. *Trail magic in the Hundred-Mile Wilderness? The sign could be old.* Happy Warrior followed me down the side trail. I recalled my first week on the trail when Soil and I headed down to our first trail magic. Now I headed to my last.

After a quarter mile, at the bottom of the road, sat a rustic cabin where two men sat on the wooden porch. Without asking, the younger of the two took out barbecue chicken and tossed it on the grill. The older man asked us if we wanted some homemade clam chowder. *Clam Chowder in the Hundred-Mile Wilderness?* While he heated the soup, the younger man explained that the older man's son had died last year.

The father came out. "My son used to cook trail magic meals."

"He was my best friend. We spread his ashes on the mountain," the younger man added.

The tight-lipped father kept the details of his son to himself.

After clam chowder, grilled chicken, and Drake's snack cakes, Happy got his pack together. I whispered in the old man's ear, "I'm carrying some of my son's ashes in my pack and plan to spread them on Katahdin."

He nodded. Up to this point no one else knew about my plan—not even Lori. To this day, I'm not sure why I kept the bottle of ashes a secret. But I wanted this father to share my experience and to know I respected his choice to honor his son's legacy. His constant gaze barely betrayed his grief, but we were in the same club.

This stoic father replayed in my head while we hiked to Long Pond Stream Lean-To. After several short climbs and sixteen miles, we stopped at the shelter where we met an older couple.

She introduced herself, "We are Mr. and Mrs. Going Home—as in going home to heaven." He was eighty-years-old, and she was in her seventies.

"Well, not tonight, I hope." Sometimes I can't help myself.

The next day the rain turned the trail into a river. A short rope spanned Pond Stream, but the swift water made the passage difficult. As I clung to the rope strung between two trees and lowered myself into the water, the torrent swept my legs out from under me. I moved hand-over-hand and regained my footing on the other side. Walking up the torrent of water that flooded the trail for eleven miles was more difficult than fording any of the wilderness streams. My shoes stuck in the mud beneath the water-filled gully. I was surprised to see them still on my feet every time I pulled them out of the muck. My shins bumped against the rocks and roots hidden under muddy water as my muscles became fatigued, leaving me exhausted and exasperated.

A steep climb to Barren Ledges led to an even steeper climb to the top of Barren Mountain. Only 2,660 feet, but I earned each foot with each sluggish step. The rain, water, cold, and almost five months on the trail made those eleven miles the toughest day on the entire trail. On this day, the Hundred-Mile Wilderness earned its reputation.

At Chair Gap Lean-to, I dropped my pack. The sun came out, revealing a beautiful evening. A young newlywed couple walked into the campsite; Ascot, tall and quiet, and Sarsaparilla, shorter and friendlier—both worked in the theater business.

"Oh, theater people," I joked, "Hey, how about a song, do you know 'Annie?' The sun will come out ..." They smiled but weren't amused. Sometimes I miss.

Later that night, another deluge ensued. Never have I seen so much rain, and never was I so glad to be in a shelter since the downpour in Virginia. The lightning and thunder closed in as the rain intensified. I hadn't seen rain like this since my third day in Georgia. When lightning lit the sky, I could see Ascot and Sarsaparilla's tent ten yards away. I was certain any minute they would make a break for the shelter, but they never did.

In the morning, they told us they took in water but just laughed about the experience. They get my John Wayne Award. He said, "Courage is being afraid but saddling up anyway."

WHEN SUNDAY SMILED

The dry day gave way to a series of satisfying climbs that culminated at White Cap Mountain, the last mountain before Katahdin. If the day had been clear, we could have seen Mount Katahdin, but we saw the same fog that had followed me from Blood Mountain in Georgia.

To make matters worse, my tablet died from collecting moisture in its protective bag. My flat piece of technology had recorded all my pictures and blogs, but fortunately my pictures up to the Hundred-Mile Wilderness were already uploaded. For the rest of the journey, I relied on my smart phone.

Happy and I continued along the trail eroded by too much water and too many hikers exposing more rocks and roots. Not to be deterred, we pushed on to Logan Brook Lean-to, which sat next to a swift-moving brook. Despite the muddy trail and the rain, I liked Maine—a lot.

After leaving Logan Brook, the trail took a gradual downhill before becoming flat. The weather and trail cooperated as we clipped off sixteen miles before 2:30 p.m. We pulled up short to regroup at a campground where we met a group from the Appalachian Long-Distance Hikers Association. The ALDHA is a non-profit group of volunteers who support the trail. They joked about their day and suggested we join their organization. Happy made an obvious overture about dinner, so later they invited us over for turkey burgers.

The next day, we covered miles of slippery roots and mud walking around Nahmakanta Lake and several ponds. I wanted to spend my last night in the wilderness alone in my tent and not snoring in a shelter.

"Go ahead without me," I told Happy. "If I find a find spot, I'm bedding down here." I was tired and hungry, but mostly tired.

"You can make it."

"Just go, I'll catch you if I can." I said before he faded in the distance. We'd already walked over twenty miles. Two days prior, I had my toughest day ever, and before that I was soaked to the core. But there was also trail magic, dinner with ALDHA, and theater folk.

I just want to sleep. I pictured myself lying down on fallen pine needles, not even bothering with my tent or my boots. But there were no spots, no Greyhound bus, no one to hear me complain. Just me. So I just walked. And after twenty-six-miles, I staggered into Rainbow Stream Lean-to where Happy had already spread his sleeping bag.

"Are there any tent sites?" I mumbled.

"I think I saw sites four miles up the trail," replied a young hiker.

I laughed when I thought about trying to hike four more miles on top of the twenty-six I'd just finished.

"You must be new," I said, as I turned to find a site. He reminded me of so many of the section-hikers I met when I first began. Happy explained to the hiker how far we came, while I found a site behind the lean-to.

I washed my socks, ate, and sat alone on a knoll overlooking the lean-to by the water's edge. Just me, a little vegetation, and a few towering trees. I finished my daily chores in the dark.

That's it? That was the wilderness? Where was the drama, the bogs that buried VW bugs, the famine, the pestilence, the drama? The drama was between my ears and it was up to me to saddle up. I fell asleep knowing the journey was worth every mile.

Happy bounded ahead the next day while I gazed at trees, twigs, leaves and branches scattered across the forest. Lichen grew on rounded rocks while overhead, birds and squirrels flitted or jumped between the trees. I cared little about my pace while I walked over small hills and across hardened mud bogs. Few insects interrupted me, quiet were the woods that settled around me.

Walking out of the Hundred-Mile Wilderness felt like waking up from a dream. With my back to the duplicate sign warning hikers about the wilderness, I stepped into the sunlight and onto a dusty road busy with noisy logging trucks and trailers carrying rubber rafts. The road and clearing lay in stark contrast to the rain-soaked woods. Abol Bridge was like an alternate universe teeming with tourists and workers. Life moved faster than me. I wanted away from the dirt road and the intimidating vehicles traveling it.

As I crossed the bridge, I got my clear view of Mount Katahdin rising in the background. The natural pyramid was close and so large. Torn between gazing at the monster that rose from the land around it or sitting down for lunch, I chose food and looked for Happy Warrior. Filled with an eagerness from being just days away, I lost myself in thoughts and struggled to make a coherent sentence. My mind slowed, and my tongue was thick. I searched for something meaningful, but nothing came to mind. Later, I wrote in my blog:

> I stepped onto a dusty road filled with logging trucks and rafting trailers. I walked alone today, and I drifted to a time when

WHEN SUNDAY SMILED

I hiked my first hike as a Stockader at Folcroft Union Church. I began to sing our childhood theme song and motto, "Bright and Keen for Christ."

I eased back into coherency when I sat down to order lunch at the campgrounds and reflected on the day. I had walked my last day with a purpose. I wanted to remember every tree, rock, and plant in the wilderness. The hundred-mile trek lived up to its reputation: the weather, the climbs, and the trail were difficult. The wilderness wasn't just a lack of roads, or people, or bridges. The wilderness was a wild gestalt. The sum of the wilderness was greater than the parts.

The trees, the views, even the water looked different each day in the wilderness. I hiked in decaying forest, new growth, and mature tree groves. I stepped over flat bogs and rocky crags. New Hampshire has the White Mountains, but Maine has the Hundred-Mile Wilderness. And Maine has Katahdin.

Maine wins.

I bought my last supplies at the campground including a hoagie I planned to eat on top of Mount Katahdin, my last meal. To keep things simple, I planned to eat half for dinner tonight and half on the mountain tomorrow.

Across the street was a state park with reasonable rates. Happy Warrior wanted to stay near the restaurant but later decided to join me. After walking to the water's edge, I met Flask who remembered meeting me at the quarter point of the trail in Tennessee. We sat with another hiker, who was a youth pastor, as darkness settled in. Flask brought up his skepticism about God and his creation.

"Let me tell you my story." I began with Aaron and ended with how God had taken care of me for the past five months in his world. *Such a change since Troutville.* In Troutville, I hesitated to share my faith with the hikers and bikers after we received food from a church picnic.

The next day my ten-mile walk to Baxter State Park unfolded as the easiest path on the A.T. The well-groomed trail had none of the mud, roots, or stones that had plagued me for the last two thousand miles. I saw no one and walked alone on soft pine needles, the first time I was alone all day during my entire hike.

After checking in at the ranger station, I walked to the Birches Lean-to where I set up my tent for the last time. Several hikers joined the site:

Happy Warrior, the extrovert; Captain K, the eccentric; and Ascot and Sarsaparilla, the theater people. Glamper, who first took my picture at McAfee Knob in Virginia, showed up but decided to summit later when his mother could join him. During his hike, he took care of Papa Al, and now he thought about his mom. Nurse, who I'd met back in Vermont, Loon, Fonz, and Easy arrived later.

Loon is an older hiker, who had hiked the Appalachian Trail multiple times. Comfortable in his own skin and in the woods, Loon's easiness made those around him just as comfortable. His sage wisdom was well-received.

Earlier in Maine, I read an article posted on the internet indicating Baxter State Park rangers were upset with backpackers. Apparently, former Governor Baxter donated most of the land and intended for the area to remain in a natural state. Now that Mt. Katahdin has become the focal point, the number of hikers and campers threatened its ecosystem.

Scott Jurak, who passed me in Pennsylvania, brought more notoriety to the park when he broke the hiking record in forty-six days, eight hours, and eight minutes. After his entourage took champagne to the top and left trash behind, the rangers cited his group for breaking several park rules. Officials also feared there would be a sharp increase in A.T. thru-hikers when the movie *A Walk in the Woods* debuted in September.

Concerns about thru-hikers at Baxter are unfounded. The majority of visitors to Katahdin are day-hikers. Thru-hikers became a target as park officials threatened to shut Mount Katahdin to the Appalachian Trail. The threat was an overreaction that got people's attention. The park, however, is crowded, and the trails are overused.

I expected to meet antagonistic rangers, but they were helpful as they showed me the way to the campsite and answered my questions. They were also involved in a search for an elderly hiker who was lost overnight.

A young ranger gave me a yellow slip of paper and said, "Congratulations."

I stared at the number, the 372nd thru-hiker to arrive at Baxter that season. The number was meaningless, but the paper was precious. The number could have been one or one million, but that piece of paper proved my pilgrimage was real. Like the scrap of paper with a medical examiner's phone number to call the day my son died, it was just paper. But that paper changed everything.

Mountain Squid said on the first day of my hike, "The last person to Katahdin wins." Getting that yellow slip of paper with my trail name

"Phantom" told me I won. I made it to the end as a thru-hiker by walking the entire trail in one year. I didn't just hike for Aaron, I hiked with him and a host of people who cared for me. Never wanting to forget the moment, I tucked the yellow paper in my backpack.

I pitched my tent on the only wooden platform at the Birches Lean-to. The Birches was restricted to thru-hikers. We joked they wanted to keep us away from the day-hikers' picnic baskets, but we cherished our solitude together. I was sitting in a locker room before the big game or in the little room beside the church sanctuary waiting for the marriage ceremony.

We were together and alone at the same time. I shared my tent platform with Sarsaparilla and Ascot while several other tents set up around the shelter for the last night. I wanted to warn them about my snoring, but it just didn't matter. Happy Warrior and Captain K, the eccentric pilot, stayed in the shelter.

During my entire hike from Georgia to Maine, I never made a fire. I collected wood for others who built a fire, but I never made one myself. I had made plenty of fires in the past, including one big one behind my house as a kid, which earned me a memorable licking. On the trail, I never stopped to build one. Happy asked the park ranger for the extra firewood in her pickup truck and gave the pile to me.

There is something magical about a fire. In Tennessee, we had a fire in the shelter when Six Strings played his ukulele. Flap Jack lit a fire in Virginia when I got my trail name, and when I shared my story with Cruise Control and Mr. Clean around a fire. Now I lit a fire on our last night in Maine. I pictured being alone on the last night, like John the Baptist with his hairy coat alone in the wilderness. But I wasn't alone, and I haven't been since I started.

We sat around the fire and talked into the night about the trail, but mostly we talked about the next day. Nurse, a nurse from Vermont, had

a booming voice that carried through the woods but seemed more sedate than usual. Easy was a young European who came here to hike the Appalachian Trail. Ascot wore a small towel around his neck. His wife, Sarsaparilla, was about a foot shorter than him. They and Captain K talked musicals.

Fonz was a young hiker who soaked up every word. The oldest hiker, Loon, had hiked the mountain several times and offered helpful advice about what to expect. His calming manner was akin to a Jedi warrior. This seasoned hiker knew the wilderness; the wild made him a better person. He called me an animal, which is a compliment in the woods. But I'm not an animal. I needed the warm fire and the people who surrounded it.

Everyone wanted to be up early. I doubted I could sleep—it was the night before Christmas. I looked out of my tent at 4:30 and saw Loon packing up his tent. He planned on hiking slow and wanted to get an early start, so he could complete the climb. Impressed with his dedication, I drifted back to sleep.

I got up at 5:15, packed up my gear, and ate the last of my Knorr noodles, which carried me through my entire trip. Anything tastes good after a twenty-mile day. My sense of taste heightened, making everything taste better. I would miss that sensation, but I was glad to see that last noodle disappear. I've never eaten them again.

With a belly full of noodles, I walked down the approach trail—the wrong approach trail. On my last day, I got to the trailhead later than everyone else and much later than I'd planned. The late start was all part of a plan, just not my plan. I would hike the mountain regardless of when I started. "It's not how you start," I reminded myself, "it's how you finish." And I would finish.

Two young park volunteers stood at the trailhead with a clipboard. They talked weather while I signed in. Their weather report didn't concern me; today was game day. I would walk up to the famed sign atop Katahdin, then I would turn around and come back down as a thru-hiker.

The first mile and a half started as a gradual climb alongside my last waterfall. I felt my lunchtime sandwich thump at the bottom of my lightened backpack. The trail turned upward as I walked around the rocks and over the roots. Maybe the adrenaline, or the ascension, or the five million steps from Georgia to Maine caused me to sweat. Maybe my adrenaline was from imagining the imposing picture of Mount Katahdin rising 5,268 feet surrounded only by foot hills. No, my exertion on this cool overcast morning came from knowing this was my last day on the A.T.

Iron rods drilled into select boulders helped lift me over the fifteen-foot natural barriers. The treacherous A.T. trail would end on a tough climb. I caught up to some day-hikers as they stopped to rearrange their goals.

They hiked in stark contrast to seasoned thru-hikers who climbed with a single-minded purpose.

Today, I found myself quiet and pressed on. My manner was in reverence to the mountain I had envisioned for the past five months, while day-hikers looked for a place to picnic on their Sunday outing. After praising a father for being out with his son, I looked up for a place to pray.

After getting to the top of another boulder, I turned around but could only see the familiar low-hanging fog hovering over the rolling countryside. I wanted a view, but the weather fit the occasion and my somber, edgy mood. Like my first step on Springer Mountain in Georgia, every step mattered.

The trail leveled off with two miles to go. Signs along the edge marked the ground as "fragile." I've been on fragile ground since the officer walked up our stone path, but now, an impromptu spring ran through tufts of grass growing between the rocks. I tried as best as I could to keep my feet dry as I straddled the puddles and pushed against the roped-off trail.

"Phantom," Nurse said, barely looking, on his way back down.

"Nurse," I replied. We bumped fists and never looked back.

"Five more minutes, Phantom," Happy Warrior said as he passed me going back down the mountain. Several others accompanied him, laughing and bounding lightly down the trail. I never saw them again.

There it was, one word—KATAHDIN. I stopped at first sight. The word took my breath and filled my senses. The understated sign burned a picture into the recesses of my memory.

KATAHDIN
BAXTER PEAK—ELEVATION—5267 FT.
NORTHERN TERMINUS OF THE
APPALACHIAN TRAIL
A MOUNTAIN FOOTPATH EXTENDING OVER
2000 MILES TO SPRINGER MOUNTAIN, GA

Easy, Ascot and Sarsaparilla were busy finishing their photo shoot.

"Phantom, you made it!" they exclaimed. I choked up, I knew I would, and went to one knee, thanking God, and remembering everyone who supported me. Around my neck, I wore my and my Lori's wooden crosses given to us in Virginia. I clutched them tightly and held onto Aaron's Keystone lift maintenance hat. Then, from out of my pocket I took the pill bottle I had been carrying for much of the trail. The vial held a few ashes, remnants from my oldest son's lifeless body. There on this special mountain, I released his dust into the wind and onto the rocks. I wept. I let him go. I was done.

Sunday, August 30, 2015. Aaron would have been thirty-two today, born August 30, 1983.

Seeing the sign was like standing in front of our Christmas tree as a child. The tree had been there for weeks—but on this morning, something was different. On this morning, it was Christmas.

Out of the hundreds of mountains lining the Appalachian Trail, including Cove Mountain in Duncannon and Killington Mountain in Vermont, Katahdin was my final mountaintop experience. Aaron was more alive in death and couldn't be a bigger part of this trip than if he had walked alongside me for every step. Because he did.

When Sarsaparilla took my picture, I told her today was Aaron's birthday. She thought it was a special way to honor his life. I sat down and, although I wasn't hungry, I ate the rest of my hoagie next to a young day hiker who asked about thru-hiking. I tried to capture the trail, but my words fell short.

I called Lori to leave her a simple message, "We did it—we." Sunday smiled.

A few minutes later, I said, "Okay, let's get a happy picture," and leaned over the sign for the classic thru-hiker pose.

I remember little about my climb down. I know returning took longer than I expected. I remember passing Loon and telling him he was the "Old Man of the Mountain." He belonged there. When I got to the bottom, people scurried about as they packed up their weekend. They were oblivious to the world I'd lived in for the last five months.

For weeks, hikers discussed their travel arrangements to get home. If I got to Maine, I wasn't worried how I would get home, so I started down the dirt road towards Millinocket. I didn't know how far the town was, but I knew I'd get there.

I stuck out my thumb. Three riders in a well-worn Subaru turned around to pick me up.

"Hey, man, I'm an ordained minister, and God told me to stop."

I looked at some of his tattoos from behind—I would be all right.

"I just need a ride into Millinocket."

After hearing me talk to Lori on the phone, he turned to me and said, "We're taking you to Bangor." Bangor was over an hour and seventy miles out of their way. My last trail angel's car sputtered down the highway. The shocks were gone, the dashboard warning lights flickered, and the front seat headrest lay at my feet. God provided a local angel who taught me how to pronounce "Bangor."

In Bangor, I rented a room and the next day checked out as a group of Navy SEALs checked in. I tried to explain to the leader I used to work with the SEALs and I'd just hiked the A.T., but it mattered little to him. We were from different worlds.

CHAPTER 17

THRU-HIKING THROUGH LIFE

I thought I was missing something after I checked in at Bangor Airport. It was my pack, already checked as baggage. My pack was now part of me, and something was wrong when my pack wasn't on my back. Both satisfaction and relief enveloped me as I flew to Denver over the same mountains I walked. I fell asleep after leaving almost everything I had on the mountain. I was spent. Lori was in Colorado with our daughter and grandson, and I wanted to be with them.

I wrote in my blog:

> After Aaron's Celebration of Life service, Aaron's closest friends Josh and Ami Stone called and asked us to stop by their house before we left. They had something special to show us.
>
> They had a cocoon in the garage left over from a school project. They had thought about throwing out the little pod because its hatch date had long passed. The day after the Celebration of Life, Josh was getting in his car and noticed something yellow moving in the corner. The butterfly had hatched the day before and bounced against the walls of its container. He belonged to the outdoors.
>
> Ami, Lori, the kids, and I took the container outside and opened it. After a few minutes, he flew to a small stick and rested in a scrub pine. This yellow wonder wasn't born for the scrubs. After getting his bearings, the Tiger Swallow Tail took off for the tallest pines in the field. First in a circle, then back and forth before resting out of reach on the highest branch. Just like

Aaron. Lori's voice quivered as she wished the butterfly well and hoped he would be safe.

Butterflies took on a new meaning for us. They showed up at key moments, letting us know they are somehow God's messengers reminding us of our son in heaven.

While we stayed in Denver, I found a butterfly house, so we took Jayden to experience some magic. We were in time to see the daily release as brightly colored butterflies were freed inside a large room filled with trees and bushes. The room smelled like a rain forest. We heard the laughter of children and watched multi-colored wings search for a place to call home. In a short time, they will fall to the ground and someone will sweep them to the side. But today, they stretched their wings to find something to eat. Today was their only concern.

I always liked butterflies, but never understood their purpose. Butterflies live about two weeks fluttering about the flowers. Some go for the highest branches, some cling to corners trying not to be noticed. They have a purpose, even if their's is a call to beauty or simply bringing a smile to mother's life.

That's purpose enough for most living things.

I held the door open as we left the butterfly house and Jayden walked through before Lori. She stopped short, turned around, and kissed me. Guess I never knew I've been kissing a butterfly all this time.

After saying goodbye to our daughter and grandson, we flew back to the coast of North Carolina.

"It looks so flat," I commented to Lori as we drove home from the airport to our house in eastern North Carolina. For the next thirty days, I found myself fatigued when climbing stairs and my joints hesitated when I walked downstairs. They seemed to whisper, "Whoa, no you don't, not again."

Even my sense of balance seemed askew, possibly because I no longer walked with a pack, or maybe because I was on flat ground. My feet shed layers of calloused skin that looked more reptilian than mammal. The dry, cracked condition was painful. *Was I walking on glass?* I'd caught a cold before leaving Maine, which hung on for more than a month. I breathed heavily and coughed up phlegm as the weakened lower half of my body tried to support me. My body told me to rest. I grew fond of midday naps. Food did not taste as good as it did on the trail, but I ate as much as I could and gained back more weight than I lost.

I found myself lethargic throughout the day. While on the trail, I made plans that gave birth to multiple dreams. Now I wanted to sleep. I've never been compulsive but anything out of place became troublesome and social events seemed awkward. I no longer felt pressured to perform, but my silence seemed unsettling for those around me.

I collected my thoughts and put them down on paper to capture everything before my memories eroded. I set a schedule to write while my body healed itself. My speech labored like tripping on roots. But my written word, once a source of motivation, now outlined my story with real-time accuracy and highlighted my lessons learned.

From start to finish, my lesson continues to be, *God's world opened when everything I needed was on my back, and my only concern was the next white blaze.*

My rainy training hikes in March started my thru-hike to who I am. I walked past who I was and got a glimpse of who I will someday be.

When I got on that Greyhound bound for Georgia, I looked around and realized that all of us were just trying to make our way through life. Grace is what emerged after reading the New Testament on the trail. Grace is the free and unmerited favor of God. It's not a coincidence that the alternate definition of grace is "simple elegance." When I embraced God's unmerited favor and practiced grace, I experienced simple elegance.

On my third day on the trail, I experienced the power of a mountain storm followed by some gracious people sharing trail magic. God's interest in every facet of my life is echoed in his embracing my son. His interest restored me in this world.

Restoration required forgiveness, and I needed to forgive the woman who took my son's life. I needed to take that pain on to let it go. My anger consumed me. I asked why, and I got no answer. I couldn't let my anger go. I wasn't just stuck, I was dying. The loss still hurts, I still grieve and get angry, but not until I forgave that I began again. Even in moments of utter frustration, God brought me back to him. God happened in the Greyson

Highlands when Lori and I struggled, and a man handed us two wooden crosses. Then another man gave us a ride back to town and told me about his son who died over thirty years before.

After the sentencing hearing, I had a newfound sense of optimism. I trusted the trail to choose a new trail name for me. I became Phantom, a solitary nomad enveloped in the blessings of community.

That's what Trail Days did for me. A young man picking up his wife at prison and an old man who spent twenty-seven years in the Navy blessed me. Townspeople dowsed me with water guns in the hiker parade. Hikers remembered me. I smiled, talked, and embraced the community. I trusted others.

When I was sick for four days in Daleville, I learned to wait on God. I hiked my hike and focused on staying positive. When walking uphill, my mood turned sour. I became patient with downhills. I practiced my motto *No Regrets*, given to me by Lori as I got on that Greyhound bus. My motto saved me from the needless mental gymnastics that use to leave me exhausted.

Above all, I learned to walk, just walk. Just walk means I take up my cross and walk knowing God's hand is on me. I will be okay. I didn't know what would happen when I walked away from Daleville after I got sick with Norovirus, but I knew I would be okay. I grew in confidence, not in myself, but in God and in my fellow hikers.

The simple traditions of jumping into the James River and eating a half-gallon of ice cream were all part of joining the community. When I hiked up Cove Mountain and looked down on Duncannon where we married and began our family, I experienced a profound blessing. I was Jimmy Stewart in *It's a Wonderful Life* as I walked down Market Street, greeting old friends as pleasant memories flooded my senses. I knew then that every day can be the best day of my life.

Those feelings replicated when I reunited with my old soccer coach, Helmut Hensel, and Aaron's friends in eastern Pennsylvania. When I needed someone, God provided. God put people in my life from the time I prayed on my second night and met Grumpy and Sleepy, to Just Greg, to Tiger Bob, Bee Stinger, and Happy Warrior.

I needed Tiger Bob at my second mountaintop experience on Killington Mountain. I would not have walked up to the summit without him. And being with him validated that special day. Not since I walked forward in church in the eighth grade have I been as close to God as that day on Killington. If God concerned himself with my tent poles, he is even more concerned about my son. God's son died on the cross—he knows anger, grief, and loss. He knows how to deal with these emotions, and he knows me. God is in my club.

Like the Israelites in the wilderness, I still doubted myself and the power of God. I worried about quitting and wondered if today would be my last. The Promised Land waited, but I wasn't ready. I worried about the White Mountains but there I was, not fifty yards from Galehead Hut at the onset of a terrific storm. Oh, how happy was I to be warm and dry amidst the thunder, lightning, and rain. Oh my! I found safe haven since my first rain storm in Trey Gap, Georgia, to my last rain drop in the Hundred-Mile Wilderness. That is nothing but miraculous.

Going from forgettable to Phantom proved more miraculous. Taking this old introvert and turning him into a friendly thru-hiker is not as dramatic as Paul's conversion on the road to Damascus, but I got stronger. I may have been tired, but my resolve strengthened with each passing state. I am stronger. I grieve and think of Aaron daily. Depression, guilt, and anger are still a part of my life. I am not over it, or past it, nor have I grown beyond it. Closure is a crock. I am not always better. I am always stronger. My strength grew on the A.T.

When I walked into the Hundred-Mile Wilderness, I was quietly confident, more so than the south-bounders who were new to the trail and espoused tall tales. In the solitude of the Wilderness, I met a man who'd lost a son yet continued his legacy by giving to others. I met similar parents in Virginia and Pennsylvania. Their message strengthened my resolve to walk.

I had five months of lessons before I fell to one knee on a Sunday morning on Mount Katahdin. A physical end to my pilgrimage. And that Sunday was my son's birthday, and my Christmas. Last Christmas, I felt lost. On this Christmas, I felt complete.

I thru-hiked the Appalachian Trail, but I desire to thru-hike through life. Unconditional love became real after my son died. Aaron's death showed me nothing else matters in life but life. Life matters—all else is vanity. I can kill relationships with trivial judgment. I need to keep relationships alive. Life is relationship. And relationship brings meaning.

Thru-hiking through life means God is more than just in my club. He gets me. He has a plan for me. I don't know what God's plan is for my life, but I know what his will is. His will is that I worship and enjoy him forever.

I am growing closer to those around me. To do this, I practice grace. Every day I pray for grace and try to display the unmerited favor God has shown toward me. That means unmerited favor toward people like Dupont who beg for food, and especially for the woman who drove in front of my son. I still smile at the trees. When they don't smile back, I remember they are not mad at me. They're trees, and that's what trees do.

Thru-hiking through life means taking up my cross and humbly walking with confidence. Everyone has a cross to bear. I have mine—I can't bear my cross alone. But I can bear it. When I got to the end of the trail, I finished reading the confusing Book of Revelation. This is what I learned—God wins. That is why I can thru-hike through life today.

It's true on the trail, it's true in life. *I begin my thru-hike through life the moment everything I own I give to God, and my only focus is on where he leads me.*

When Aaron was just a baby, we bundled him up, and I held him in my arms as I made my way to the car for church. Just early winter, but snow and ice lay on the ground. As I reached for the door, I slipped on the ice, lost my footing and fell, cradling our son. On the ground, I hesitated before looking inside the bundle. Aaron looked back at me, smiling as if nothing had happened.

I knew then, Aaron wasn't mine—he was God's. I was his steward, charged with taking care of him. I held on to him when we hit the ice, and when I got up, I gave him to God. He never was mine, but I never wanted to let him go. When I gave him to God, Sunday smiled.

ONE

One blaze one step
One mile one life
One 3 x 6 but one at a time.
One fall one rise,
One climb and one loss
One time I quit
One time I lost
And one time I thought
I was lost
But one time One found me again
One reached down,
One picked me up
One breathed new life
And One laid me down
My eyes are on One
One time, one mark
One man walking in the dark
Yet one man walking to the fight
Walking to hope, wanting to die
One
One more time, try as I might

—Davidson

ABOUT THE AUTHOR

Andy Davidson grew up in the working-class suburbs of South Philadelphia. In his diverse neighborhood, everyone knew whose kid you were, and you had to be home by the time the street lights came on. He grew up going to church on Sunday, playing little league, and taking out the trash on Tuesdays. As a twin in a family of five with his grandmother who lived upstairs, Andy was surrounded by family. His main interest at the time was watching Batman and playing sports. Football and baseball were later replaced with soccer and wrestling. After graduating from the Christian Academy in Chester, Pennsylvania, he went on to play soccer and major in Behavioral Sciences at Messiah College.

As a student, Andy met his wife Lori, and the couple were married on her family farm in Perry County after graduation. They raised their three children, Aaron, Ali, and Robby in Duncannon alongside their sheep, goats, and horses. When Andy decided to return to school, they packed up their children, all under the age of five, and moved to Indiana. He studied Clinical Psychology at Indiana State University then accepted a commission in the US Navy to complete his doctorate degree. During his twenty-one-year career, Captain Davidson deployed with Navy SEALs and Army Special Operations in Afghanistan and Iraq.

After retiring from the US Navy, he and Lori settled on the coast in North Carolina. Andy made plans to hike the Appalachian Trail and expected that Aaron, age thirty, would join him. However, when Aaron was killed while riding a motorcycle in 2014, everything changed.

That is when I realized that despite my faith in God, my education as a Clinical Psychologist, and my experience with dealing with warriors who experienced great loss, I learned I knew nothing.

From this moment, his writing, his speaking, and his website have been dedicated to the thousands of parents, who like Andy, continue to search for answers to life's most difficult questions.

SCRIPTURE REFERENCES:

1. Page 19—Matthew 5:45
2. Page 44—John 3:16
3. Page 49—Revelation 3:16
4. Page 74—Matthew 16:24
5. Page 94—Proverbs 27:17a
6. Page 117—John 21:17
7. Page 135—2 Corinthians 1:9

Made in the USA
Columbia, SC
07 October 2020